TEACHER'S GUIDE

1001 Nights Language & Literacy Lesson Plans

BIG BAD BOO PRODUCTIONS

CHILDREN'S GLOBAL NETWORK

THE EDUCATION AND DIVERSITY FOUNDATION

www.bigbadboo.com

1001 NIGHTS ADAPTATION

Aly Jetha, Shabnam Rezaei,
and Randy Rogel

PROGRAM ADVISORS AND EXPERTS

Dr. Raza Ali Abidi, Hon. PhD., Bahawalpur University
Dr. Muhammad Aslam Adeeb, PhD., Bradford University
Mehnaz Akber Aziz, MA, University of Sussex
Jordan Brown, MA, Columbia University
Dr. Sholly Fisch, Ph.D., New York University
Aly Jetha, J.D., University of California, Berkeley
Ali Moeen, MA, Bahawalpur University
Aisha Osman, BA, Cairo University

1001 NIGHTS SCHOLARS

Dr. Paulo Horta – NYU Abu Dhabi
Dr. Martyn Oliver – American University

CONTENTS

PROGRAM OVERVIEW

How to Use this Guide

This program is an interactive course that uses video, storytelling, discussions and activities as the primary methods of teaching literature and language. It also includes additional educational objectives, like teaching respect, non-violence, empathy and the importance of education.

Each lesson plan is based on a story from *1001 Nights*. Therefore, in addition to this teaching guide, teachers of this course should have (1) a set of *1001 Nights* DVDs, and (2) a *1001 Nights* Teacher's Companion Storybook. The DVDs contain animated versions of each *1001 Nights* story, and the Companion Storybook has a written version of each *1001 Nights* story in the course. Teachers who do not have access to a TV and DVD player should use the Companion Storybook to read the stories to their students instead of having them watch the DVD. Those who do have access to a TV and DVD player can either play the episode on the DVD or read the story from the storybook.

Activity Sheets

The *1001 Nights Student Activity Book* is available for students to purchase. This Course Book contains all in-class activity sheets and take-home assignments for the course.

If students are unable to purchase Course Books, teachers must make copies of the activity sheets (located at the end of each lesson plan) for their students' use prior to each class. In some cases, the activity sheets are required for in-class activities, and in other cases, the activity sheets are required for take-home assignments.

LESSON PLANS

Each lesson plan has been structured in the same way and follows the same format with the following contents:

<u>Story Summary</u> – This has been provided for teachers to review prior to class, to refresh them on important points of the story for the day's lesson plan.

<u>Story Lessons</u> – A list of story lessons is provided for teachers to review prior to class.

<u>Class Plans</u>

The Class Plan is the suggested outline of activities to teach the class. Each lesson plan has four sets of activities. Each lesson may be taught in 25-30 minutes or 50-60 minutes. The 25-30 minute classes will only undertake the first three activities listed below. Classes that are 50-60 minutes long will do all four activities listed below.

FIRST ACTIVITY – PRE-VIEWING DISCUSSION/EXERCISE (5-10 minutes)
Each class begins with an exercise or discussion that should be undertaken before the students view, or are read, the *1001 Nights* story for the day. The purpose of this activity is to introduce the story or an important concept from the educational objectives.

SECOND ACTIVITY – WATCH EPISODE (10 minutes)
After the pre-viewing exercise, teachers should play the associated episode of *1001 Nights* from the DVD, or read the story to the students from the Companion Storybook.

THIRD ACTIVITY – POST VIEWING DISCUSSION (10 minutes)
After viewing or listening to the story, teachers are to engage students in a discussion about the story and certain important points. The lesson plans provide suggested topics for discussion, however, teachers should feel free to create their own discussion points or let students ask questions they feel are interesting.

FOURTH ACTIVITY – IN-CLASS EXERCISE/ACTIVITY (20-30 minutes)
Only for classes that are 50-60 minutes long. The 25-30 minute classes will omit this activity.

<u>Activity Sheets</u>

At the end of each lesson plan are between one to three activity sheets. *These sheets may be required for in-class activities or as take-home assignments.* As such, if students have not purchased Course Books, *teachers will need to make copies of the activity sheets for all their students prior to class.*

COURSE INTRODUCTION

In the first class, prior to teaching the first lesson, teachers should introduce their students to *1001 Nights*.

About *1001 Nights*

1001 Nights is one of the most famous collections of stories of all time. The stories were originally told more than a thousand years ago by Shahrzad, the queen and wife of King Shahryar. Legend has it that on their wedding night, Shahrzad began telling Shahryar a story and did not finish it. The king was so enraptured by the story that he commanded her to finish the story the following night. The next night, Shahrzad finished her original story and began another, which again she did not finish. As before, the king was so enraptured that he again asked her to finish her story the next night. This continued for 1,001 nights.

As a young child, Shahrzad loved to read, and her father brought her books from all over the world. Her knowledge made her a magical storyteller and a great teacher. She was especially well-known for her ability to wisp a story out of the air to resolve any dispute. Her stories have been told and retold by storytellers for more than a thousand years.

In this class, students will study 1001 Nights and will, hopefully, like many who have heard them over time, be entertained and learn from Shahrzad's stories.

The characters of *1001 Nights* include:

Queen Shahrzad – the wife of King Shahryar and the storyteller
King Shahryar – the king of the court
Donyazad – Shahrzad's younger sister, who is nine years old
Prince Shahzaman – King Shahryar's younger brother, who is ten years old
Majid – King Shahryar's vizier, who also happens to be Donyazad and Shahrzad's father
Maymoon – Shahzaman and Donyazad's pet monkey

TRUE TREASURE

Story Summary

Shahryar is bored and walks around his castle complaining that he can't find anything fun or interesting to do. When Shahzaman and Donyazad ask if he would like to go hiking or swimming, he says that he's busy trying to find something fun to do. This inspires Shahrzad to tell him this story:

Mujab is jealous because his neighbor is rich and has nicer things. Mujab wishes that he were rich. That night, he has a dream in which a white bird tells him his treasure awaits him inside a palace. Since the only palaces around are in Cairo, Mujab sets off for Cairo on his donkey. Enduring hardships, he finally arrives in Cairo, where he is arrested and imprisoned for a crime he didn't commit. While in jail, he makes a new friend named Samir, who had the same dream and was also arrested for a crime he did not commit. Together they make a daring escape, find a castle, and sneak inside to locate their treasure, only to run afoul of the police once again. They escape once more with their lives, but this time they wind up lost in the desert, stranded without water and near death. As Mujab lies there preparing to die, he realizes what the dream really meant: *His home was his castle, and the true treasure was his family.* Lamenting his folly, he is saved at the last moment by his faithful donkey, who takes him and Samir back home.

Story Lessons
- Encourage children to identify and appreciate all the simple "treasures" they already have, especially their family and friends.
- Help children understand that greed and materialism can be blinding, and that obsessing over material goods can be harmful and lead to a very unfulfilling life.

CLASS PLAN

Pre-Viewing Activity (Approximately 5 Minutes)

Before showing the video of "True Treasure" (or reading the storybook version), ask the students to write on a piece of paper the most valuable things they have in life and cannot live without. Once they have had a few minutes to write them down, the teacher should ask the students to name some of the things they have listed and write them on the board.

Tell the students that in this episode, a man named Mujab goes on a treasure hunt to a big palace in Cairo. Ask them to brainstorm what sorts of treasure they would like to find if they were Mujab and write some of the ideas on the board.

Watch or Read Episode (Approximately 10 Minutes)

Post-Viewing Discussion Questions (Approximately 10 Minutes)

In the end, what did Mujab think the most valuable treasure was? Why?
(*Discussion:* Mujab realizes that his family is his true treasure and that it was with him his entire life. He realizes that by envying his neighbor's possessions, and leaving his family in search of riches, he made himself unhappy.)

When you look at the list of items on the board, what do you think are the most important treasures in life?
(*Discussion:* Discuss the difference between material goods and non-material goods. True happiness usually comes from meaningful time spent with friends and family.)

Let's pretend that you have a new football and one of your friends felt left out because he or she didn't have (or could not afford) one. What should you do?
(*Discussion:* We could play together. Having a football and playing on your own is less fun than sharing and playing with friends.)

In-Class Activity – for 50-60 Minute Lessons (Approximately 30 Minutes)

"NEEDS VS. WANTS": In this episode, Mujab is jealous of his neighbor's possessions. Even when his neighbor generously offers to share (such as inviting his family over for a barbeque), Mujab is rude and turns him away. Discuss: At the start of the episode, what did Mujab think he wanted? By the end, what did he discover he really needed? What is the difference between "wanting" and "needing" something?

Ask students to imagine they are explorers who are going to a faraway place where no one else lives. They can bring anything they want on the trip, but they can only bring five things. If they could bring any five items with them, what would they choose? Write all suggestions on the board, and then ask students to evaluate each of the items, and decide if it is a "want" or a "need." Encourage students to realize that needs are the things they would need for basic human survival—food, water, shelter, clothing, medicine, friends, family and so on. Which items could they live without?

ACTIVITY ONE: DIGGING FOR REAL TREASURES

What are the true treasures in your life? In the open space, draw three of your favorite things to do with your friends or family.

LESSON ONE

TAKE-HOME ACTIVITY

NAME: _____

ACTIVITY TWO: TRUE TREASURES & FALSE FORTUNES

At the beginning of the episode "True Treasure", Shahryar is looking for something fun and exciting to do. Shahrzad tells him that often what people are looking for is right there in front of them. What does she mean by this?

Below, Shahryar is trying to find things that will make him happy. Can you help him by circling activities or things that are true treasures and cross out the false fortunes? Then use the empty boxes to draw other true treasures that will make him (and you) happy.

TAKE-HOME ACTIVITY

NAME: _____

WHAT'S YOURS IS MINE

Note: Prior to class, teachers will need to make one copy of Activity Sheet One. Teachers will also need to have one dice, which will be used for the extended In-Class Activity.

Story Summary

When Shahzaman and Donyazad fight over a ring they find, Shahrzad warns them of the perils of greed by telling this story:

When a poor fisherman catches a mermaid and lets her go, the mermaid gives him a pearl as a gift for his kindness. When the emperor sees the pearl, he demands to buy it, but the fisherman refuses to sell. Before the emperor takes it, his vizier stops him, telling him he cannot just take the pearl because that would be against the law, and everyone must obey the law, or else there will be anarchy. The vizier and the emperor devise another way to get the pearl, which is legal. They demand that tax be paid on the pearl, which they know the fisherman cannot afford to pay. The fisherman agrees, provided he can pay the tax in fish. The emperor agrees, and just as the fisherman is about to fail, his mermaid appears and provides 1001 fish. Furious, the emperor says the fisherman has failed and demands more tasks of the fisherman. Each time, the mermaid saves the fisherman. Finally, the emperor demands the fisherman give the emperor the pearl or a mermaid. The fisherman is distraught and agrees to hand over his pearl until the mermaid demands to be taken to the emperor. Believing he has won, the emperor demands the mermaid produce a massive pearl for him. The mermaid does, and as the emperor reaches to grab it, the mermaid traps him in a large oyster shell, where he can never bother the fisherman again. In the end, the emperor learns he cannot manipulate his subjects, and that greed will wind up destroying you.

Story Lessons
- Inspire children to appreciate the importance of fairness.
- Encourage children to understand why everyone, even powerful leaders, must obey the law.
- Help children value friends and loved ones more than material objects.

CLASS PLAN

Pre-Viewing Activity (Approximately 5 Minutes)

Explain that the students will watch (or have read to them) a *1001 Nights* story that deals with the topic of fairness. Ask students to explain what the words "fair" and "unfair" mean, and to give a few examples. Then show the class an edible treat (or a picture of one) that students would find appealing and could be divided among classmates in a straightforward way.

On the board write "Unfair" and "Fair." Ask students first to think of an **unfair** way of dividing the edible treat among the students in the class. A student might suggest that he or she should get all of the treats, or all boys receive larger portions of the treat than girls, or anyone under a certain height gets an extra portion. Discuss what it would feel like if one of the unfair methods were used. Then ask students to think of **fair** ways to divide the treat among the students. Encourage children to think of as many creative solutions as possible. Then ask students how they would feel this time, if one of the fair methods were used.

Watch or Read Episode (Approximately 10 Minutes)

Post-Viewing Discussion Questions (Approximately 10 Minutes)

Do you think it was fair or unfair of the emperor to want to take the pearl from Jianyu? Why?
(*Discussion:* It was unfair because the pearl belonged to Jianyu. He should not have had to sell or give it away if he did not want to. The emperor did not have the right to use his position to force Jianyu to give him the pearl – this is misuse of his power.)

How did you feel when the emperor kept changing the rules by telling Jianyu that he failed because the fish were dead or the figs were wet? Was that fair or unfair? Why?
(*Discussion:* The emperor was being unfair. The emperor was changing the rules to try to cheat Jianyu. He asked Jianyu to bring him fish and figs, but he never said anything about the fish needing to be alive or the figs needing to be dry.)

Why did the vizier tell the emperor that he could not just take the pearl from Jianyu?
(*Discussion:* Because taking the pearl would be stealing, which is against the law. Have students explain why the emperor should not break the law, or why it is not fair to have a law apply differently to different people – even those in positions of power.)

The vizier told the emperor he must follow the law. Do emperors have to obey the law? Why? What happens if the law doesn't apply to the emperor?
(*Discussion:* The purpose of having laws is usually to bring order to a group of people, so that everyone is as safe and happy as possible. For example, the purpose of a speed limit while driving a car is to keep everyone safe on the road. If the emperor could drive his car at any speed he wanted, he might drive too fast, which might injure himself or other drivers.)

In-Class Activity – for 50-60 Minute Lessons (Approximately 30 Minutes)

Ask for three volunteers to play a game. Present a copy of Emperor Chang's Game, which is provided as Activity One below on the next page. Teachers will also need to provide one die for use in the game.

Have the volunteers play the game where each take turns rolling the die, moving that number of places on the die and following the rules of the board. The first to the end wins. After the game, ask the three players if they would like to play again. Do the two people who lost want another chance to beat the winner?

Ask for three more volunteers to play the game. This time, however, we are going to change one thing. Each player is told they are Player One, Two, or Three, and that Player One is Jianyu, Player Two is the vizier, and Player Three is Emperor Chang. Then explain:

- When Jianyu rolls the die, he moves the exact number of places as the number on the die.
- When the vizier roles, he moves two times the number on the die.
- When Emperor Chang roles, he moves three times the number on the die.

At the end of the game, ask how they felt about the rules. Do the two who lost feel like playing the game again?

Have a class discussion on why games have rules. How do you know if the rules are fair for all? Why should the rules apply to everyone equally, even those in power?

1.
2.
Move 1 More
3.
4.
Move 2 More
5.
Lose A Turn
6.
7.
Move 3 More
8.
9.
Move Back 2
10.
Lose A Turn
11.
12.
Move 2 More
13.
14.
15.
Move Back 1
16.
17.
Move 3 More
18.
19.
Move 2 More
20.
21.
22.
Move Back 1
23.
Move Back 2
24.
Move 2 More
25.
Winner
Start

ACTIVITY TWO: FAMILY RULES

Rules work best when they are fair, everyone agrees to them, and there are positive consequences for following them. Meet with your family to come up with some rules to try out for the next week. Post them on the wall in a place where everyone will see them. At the end of the week, talk about what rules worked and which ones need to be revisited.

Homework:

RULE: If I complete my homework on time, I will get to … _____

Meal Time:

RULE: If I help with cooking and cleaning, I will get to … _____

Bed Time:

RULE: If I get ready for bed and brush my teeth by myself, then I get to…

_____

Behavior:

RULE: If I am caught misbehaving, then …

_____

Create Your Own Rule:

RULE: If _____ then…

_____

TAKE-HOME ACTIVITY

NAME: _____

CREATURE KARMA

Story Summary

Shahryar and Shahzaman make fun of Maymoon, who is upset by their taunting. When Donyazad tells them to stop, they laugh, saying he's only a monkey and has no feelings. Shahrzad tells them this story:

A young girl named Ashianna goes fishing with her father and catches a huge fish. Her father excitedly goes to find his friends, to show them his daughter's big catch. In the meantime, Ashianna feels sorry for the fish and throws it back into the water. When her father returns with his friends, he's embarrassed and angry to find that the fish is gone. He concludes fishing is not for girls. Upset, Ashianna leaves. On her walk, she comes upon a starving bird that is gagging on a ring he tried to eat. She removes the ring, and realizes she can sell it. With the money, she can buy food for the bird and give what's left over to her father, to make him proud of her. On their way to sell the ring, they meet a monkey and a panther, both of whom are in distress, and Ashianna helps them both. To their surprise, a genie comes out of the ring and grants Ashianna's wish to make the panther's cage disappear. Just as they are about to make a second wish, the panther's animal trainer steals the ring and wishes that the genie make him the sultan.

At his command, the trainer, the ring, and the genie are gone and now reside in the sultan's palace. Ashianna and her new animal friends break into the palace and recover the ring. While making a getaway, the ring falls overboard into the ocean. Just when all seems lost, the fish that Ashianna set free shows up with the ring. Proving that good deeds provide good fortune, the fish gives the ring back to Ashianna. Without needing to make another wish, Ashianna, her parents, the monkey, the panther, the bird, and the fish become one big happy family.

Story Lessons
- Teach children the concept of empathy.
- Encourage children to be aware of, and respectful of, one another's feelings.
- Help children understand that doing good deeds is the right thing to do, and often leads to good fortune.
- Help children understand that being cruel to others is wrong. We should treat people and other creatures the way that we would like to be treated.

CLASS PLAN

Pre-Viewing Activity (Approximately 5 Minutes)

Ask children to imagine they found a magical object, such as a lamp a ring. The object will grant them three wishes. What would they wish for? After the kids suggest different things to wish for, ask how they would feel about giving away a wish. Ask: What if you met one person who really needed one wish, would you give them one of yours? What if you met two people who really needed a wish? Would you give each of them one of yours and keep only one? What if you met three people who really needed help? Would you give away all of your wishes? Introduce the concept of empathy and generosity; putting yourself in someone else's shoes and putting their needs before your own.

Watch or Read Episode (Approximately 10 Minutes)

Post-Viewing Discussion Questions (Approximately 10 Minutes)

Why is it important to treat others with kindness and respect?
(*Discussion:* It is always good to treat others with respect. It makes them feel good and can make you feel good, too. If you do this, others will treat you and other people better, which leads to a better community and society.)

Why did Ashianna throw the big fish back into the water and then help the bird, the monkey and the panther? Did she want something in return?
(*Discussion:* She felt that each of these creatures was suffering and felt sorry for them. She was not hoping to get anything in return, but she built a better life for everyone and herself because she empathized with these creatures.)

Do you believe that good deeds result in good fortunes? What does this mean?
(*Discussion:* Good deeds make everybody treat one another better, which is good for society. Whether you get something directly in return or not, helping others is the right thing to do, and at a minimum, can make you feel very good.)

In-Class Activity – for 50-60 Minute Lessons (Approximately 30 Minutes)

If you have not done so already, introduce the word *empathy*. Make sure the children understand what this concept means, and offer metaphors to aid understanding. When you empathize with someone, you try to see the world through their eyes, or "put yourself in their shoes." The following is a role-playing exercise. Use the following situations to help the students think about what they can do. Feel free to create new and different situations.

1. A person in your class often feels left out and is quieter than others. What can you do?
2. There's a new student in school who is a different color/race/religion. What can you do?
3. The teacher tells the class they can go play for half an hour. Whatever you play, everyone has to do the same activity. There are three different opinions on which activity most people would enjoy. How do you resolve this?
4. You come to school, and a friend has forgotten his/her lunch. What can you do?

Now discuss why empathy is important. People get along better. People are happier. People can live together, despite being different or having different interests.

ACTIVITY ONE: THE NEW KID'S SHOES?

It's really tough being the new kid in school.

Mohammad is new in the boys' school and Ashianna is new in the girls' school. Neither have any friends and both come from a different country, speak a different language, and practice a different religion. First, make a list of five things that make Ashianna's or Mohammad's lives in the new schools challenging. Then list five things you can do to help them deal with these challenges.

Five things that make Ashianna's or Mohammad's lives in their new schools challenging:

1. _____
2. _____
3. _____
4. _____
5. _____

Five things you can do to help them deal with these challenges:

1. _____
2. _____
3. _____
4. _____
5. _____

TAKE-HOME ACTIVITY

NAME: _____

Directions: One day, the teacher walks in and says, "Today we are going to cancel class and go play in the school yard. There's one catch, everyone has to play together." The class is half an hour long. You and your friends want to play football, some other kids want to play hide-and-seek, and some others want to play handball (or another game). Write a short piece below about what you should do. If you can't agree, then you must go back to class.

_____

_____

_____

_____

_____

_____

_____

_____

_____

TO HATCH A THIEF

Story Summary

When Shahrzad catches Shahzaman and Maziar stealing cookies, the boys quickly turn on each other, each saying it was the other's idea. Shahrzad tells them this story:

In a small village near Baghdad, times have gotten so hard that men of the village begin resorting to highway robbery in order to make ends meet. One day, they rob an old man in a wagon and take his chest of gold. Dividing up the coins, they head back home, delighted with their good fortune. None of them trust one another now, so each hides their gold to protect it. Soon, fear and mistrust begin to spread among the townspeople. Many begin accusing their neighbors and friends of trying to steal from them. Locks go up on doors and bars go up on windows. The town descends into bickering and fighting until all civility breaks down. Just as the people are about to come to blows, the old man they robbed appears before them. He reveals himself to be the great King Harun al Rashid. He tells them he heard things were difficult for them, and that's why he was bringing the chest of gold, to help them! Unfortunately, they stole it from him before he could give it to them. Embarrassed, they ask why he didn't tell them who he was before. He says he wanted them to learn a lesson: *The price you pay for stealing is that no one can trust you, and you can't trust anyone else.* The townspeople apologize and give him back his money, embracing one another and becoming friends once more.

Story Lessons
- Teach children to respect others' property and understand why stealing is wrong.
- Help children understand the consequences of stealing. When a theft occurs in a community, everyone trusts one another a little less.
- If you steal, you may have more money, but you are far worse off because you will live in a society where nobody can trust or rely on one another.

CLASS PLAN

Pre-Viewing Activity (Approximately 5 Minutes)

The teacher starts the lesson by telling the students to think about a certain situation and asking how they would react. The situation is that they go to a store and buy something. The store owner accidentally gives them too much change. What would they do?

After listening to the students, the teacher should highlight that there are two options: (1) take the money and don't say anything, or (2) tell the store owner he or she has made a mistake and give him or her back the amount of money they accidentally gave the student.

Ask the students how it feels to have someone point out an honest mistake to them.

Watch or Read Episode (Approximately 10 Minutes)

Post-Viewing Discussion Questions (Approximately 10 Minutes)

Have any of you had anything stolen from you? How did it make you feel? If you haven't had anything stolen from you, how do you think it would feel?
(*Discussion:* When someone steals from you, you feel angry and distrustful of others. Sometimes the victim wants to steal something back from the person who stole from them.)

How do simple acts of honesty and dishonesty affect the community?
(*Discussion:* When people are honest, everybody trusts one another and can live more safely and happily.)

Imagine this situation: You find something at the playground, like money, a watch, a wallet, someone's lunch, etc. You know it doesn't belong to you. What should you do? Why? If you lost something, what would you want someone who found it to do?
(*Discussion:* It would be best to turn it in to the school because if I were the one who lost something, I would want it to be turned in, so I could get it back.)

Why do people steal? Do those reasons make it right, or is stealing still wrong?
(*Discussion:* People steal because they need or want something they cannot have. They also think it is okay, because they see others steal or cheat to get ahead. Other people stealing does not make it right. When you steal, you are taking something that does not belong to you, and that is wrong.)

In-Class Activity – for 50-60 Minute Lessons (Approximately 30 Minutes):

Pick two children. Give one of them a card and tell them it represents a bag of coins. Hand another student a card and tell them it represents a new bicycle. Ask them how they feel. Ask what they will do with the coins and the bicycle.

Now tell both students they need to give the cards back to the teacher. The teacher then tells them that he or she has stolen them, and they are no longer theirs.

Discuss how it feels to have something stolen from you. Discuss: Why is stealing wrong? It shows a lack of respect and caring for others, and it creates a community of distrust.

ACTIVITY ONE: *CAUGHT!*

Read this comic about Mujab and Samir and answer the questions in the open panels.

NAME: _____

THE TALE OF TWO GENIES

Story Summary

Donyazad and Shahzaman are fighting and decide to draw a line across their room. Neither may go on the other's side. When Shahrzad sees this, she tells them the following story:

A weary traveler named Mahmood is crossing the desert when he comes across a bottle and a lamp, buried in the sand. When he opens them, two genies pop out, who look nearly identical, but for some reason hate each other. They immediately begin to fight with each other, and Mahmood has to order them to stop. After repeatedly trying to get them to work together, Mahmood learns that the genies and their ancestors have hated one another for more than 1,500 years, due to petty family squabbles, which ultimately boiled down to perceived differences between "bottle" and "lamp" genies. Lamp and bottle genies are just different. They have never gotten along and never will. When they continue to fight, Mahmood has no choice but to order them back into their bottle and lamp. Mahmood drops the bottle and lamp back into the sand and rides away, hoping that someday they'll get over their differences and learn to live in peace.

Story Lessons
- Encourage children to resolve conflicts creatively and constructively, in an effort to try to get along with others.
- Help children understand that when people or groups hold onto grudges, everyone loses, as this behavior only leads to greater conflict and unhappiness.
- Fighting is a bad way to resolve disputes and, quite often, only leads to more fighting without resolving differences.
- It is important to resolve conflicts right away. The longer a conflict lasts, the longer it takes to resolve.

CLASS PLAN

Pre-Viewing Activity (Approximately 5 Minutes)

Ask students to think of a time they argued with a friend or a sibling. Suggest they pick an example in which one person accidentally did something to someone else, to which the other person responded with anger? How did they stop fighting and make up?

Have a short discussion about the following: When someone does something to offend or bother you, what *positive* options do you have? A positive reaction is one that does not make the situation worse. Some suggestions students might offer for resolving conflicts include apologizing, taking turns, agreeing to start again, and so on.

Watch or Read Episode (Approximately 10 Minutes)

Post-Viewing Discussion Questions (Approximately 5-10 Minutes)

Why did Donyazad and Shahzaman fight? Was it worth fighting? If Shahzaman had reacted differently, would they have been fighting?
(*Discussion:* Donyazad's ball accidentally knocked over Shahzaman's castle. Instead of starting an argument, Shahzaman could have asked Donyazad why she did that. She could then have responded that it was an accident and that she was sorry. Shahzaman could have politely asked Donyazad to help fix the castle. If this had happened, they could have gone back to playing nicely, without fighting.)

Was it right for Shahzaman to draw a line in the room? Why? Why not? How did Donyazad react? Was this a good reaction or a bad reaction?
(*Discussion:* Shahzaman reacted out of anger, and his reaction caused Donyazad to get angry. Both of them could have acted differently to resolve the problem.)

In the future, if Donyazad and Shahzaman start to fight, what are some positive ways they can work out their differences?
(*Discussion:* They can both take the time to calm down, maybe counting slowly to twenty, or taking deep breaths. They might apologize for their own behavior and say they'd like to do something fun together.)

If you were one of the genies, what would you do to stop fighting with the other one?
(*Discussion:* The genies could focus on all the ways they are similar. They could focus on how much better it feels to have friends than enemies and think of magical things they can do together.)

What happened when the genies stopped fighting and worked together? What happened when they began fighting again? What did they gain by fighting and what did they lose? Were they better off fighting or resolving their disputes?
(*Discussion:* When the genies were fighting, they were locked inside a bottle and a lamp, and when they got along, they created paradise. When they fought again, they lost everything, even their freedom. Getting along was much better than fighting.)

In-Class Activity – for 50-60 Minute Lessons (Approximately 30 Minutes)

In the heat of a dispute, it is sometimes difficult to respond rationally, positively, or creatively. That's why it is useful to practice effective conflict resolution with pretend scenarios. Tell each class member to find a partner for the following exercise, where one student will be Student One and the other will be Student Two.

Tell them that Student One doesn't like anybody using his or her things without permission. When Student One leaves the room one day, he or she comes back to find Student Two using his or her pen and becomes very angry. Student Two doesn't think he or she was doing anything wrong by borrowing Student One's pen and that Student One is getting angry for no reason.

Ask Student One and Student Two to discuss the issue. After five minutes, have them switch roles and try to resolve the issue again. Then have all the students sit back down in their chairs and discuss what happened. Have a discussion about the different ways Student One could react and how this makes the problem go away or makes the problem worse. Discuss the same for how Student Two could react to the different reactions of Student One and how Student Two's reaction can make the problem go away or get worse. Discuss how the reactions of both parties in any dispute contribute to whether a conflict persists or gets resolved.

ACTIVITY ONE: THE MAGIC OF ENDING CONFLICTS PEACEFULLY

LESSON FIVE

Directions: Create a poster that lists good ideas to make sure your conflicts don't turn into fights. We've helped you with the first one.

Thanks for understanding!

1.

3.

5.

TAKE-HOME ACTIVITY

NAME: _____

At the end of the story, the two genies are still arguing with each other. Now is your chance to think about how these genies can finally end their families' ancient argument and write a story that resolves their conflict.

One morning, the two genies were fighting again as usual... _____

_____

_____

_____

_____

_____

_____

_____

_____

_____

_____

Do you really think we can stop fighting...um, pal?

Sure... um, friend. I have some ideas we can try.

NAME: _____

KING BIKHARD

Story Summary

When Shahryar orders his pet monkey, Maymoon, to be thrown into the dungeon for stealing a banana, the children protest. Shahrzad tells them a story about another king who learned that laws must be reasonable, and the importance of forgiveness and clemency.

King Bikhard has huge teeth and no sense of humor. When a visiting messenger makes fun of his teeth, Bikhard orders the man arrested and thrown in prison. The messenger begs for forgiveness, and because he convinces Bikhard he meant no harm, the king forgives him and sets him free. Years later, when Bikhard's ship sinks, he ends up stranded on a distant island, where he is brought before King Coco and charged with trespassing. As King Coco is about to send him to prison, his jester appears. King Coco's court jester happens to be the messenger King Bikhard set free years ago. Returning the act of kindness, the jester convinces King Coco that sentencing Bikhard to prison is an unreasonably harsh punishment for the crime of trespassing, and that Bikhard is a good and magnanimous king who deserves mercy for having set him free years ago. King Coco is swayed by the Jester's arguments and orders Bikhard released.

Story Lessons
- Inspire children to forgive and to be kind to others.
- Encourage children to have a sense of humor about themselves and realize no one is perfect. In fact, it is our differences that make the world a more interesting place.
- Help children understand what makes a law or rule "reasonable," and realize you can sometimes stand up to unreasonable laws or rules.

CLASS PLAN

Pre-Viewing Activity (Approximately 5 Minutes)

Tell the students they are about to hear the story of King Bikhard, who has very big teeth. He's so sensitive about his teeth that if anyone mentions them, even by accident, they will be thrown into prison! What do you think of that law? After students offer responses, ask if that rule seems fair to them. Introduce the word "reasonable". Explain that reasonable laws are balanced. Explain that by "balanced" we mean that the punishment must fit the "crime." It isn't too gentle and not too harsh. Tell students that when they watch (or listen to) the story, they should look for examples of laws that are "unreasonable."

Watch or Read Episode (Approximately 10 Minutes)

Post-Viewing Discussion Questions (Approximately 10 Minutes)

Was it right or wrong for people to make jokes about King Bikhard's teeth? Why?
(*Discussion:* No, because making jokes about someone's physical appearance is not respectful and could hurt his or her feelings.)

Was it fair that King Bikhard put people in jail if they made jokes about his large teeth? What should King Bikhard have done instead?
(*Discussion:* No, it was not fair for the King to punish people for commenting on his teeth. Even if the king's feelings were hurt by the comment, putting people in jail for making fun of him is not reasonable.)

Was it fair that Shahryar wanted to throw Maymoon, the monkey, into the dungeon for stealing a banana? Why or why not? What should Shahryar have done instead?
(*Discussion:* No, throwing the monkey into the dungeon was too harsh a punishment for an animal instinctively taking a banana or joking around with Shahryar.)

Shahrzad says, "Justice must be reasonable." What does this mean?
(*Discussion:* In order for people to want to follow laws, they need to be fair. In other words, if the laws are too strict, people won't follow them and will have less respect for the leader who made them.)

Would King Bikhard think the laws were reasonable if he were the one joking about someone else's physical appearance? What does this tell you about the law?
(*Discussion:* Probably not. He is taking advantage of the fact that he is king. In a free society, the laws come from the people; they apply equally to everyone, and nobody is above the law.)

In-Class Activity – for 50-60 Minute Lessons (Approximately 30 Minutes)

First, have students work in pairs or small groups to come up with a new law they think should be followed in school. Have them propose a reasonable consequence if someone breaks this law. Then have the groups share their ideas and discuss if they agree that the laws and the consequences are reasonable.

ACTIVITY ONE: OUR FAMILY'S "REASONABLE" RULES LESSON SIX

Directions: Work with your family to come up with five new laws that will hopefully make life at home happier. All the rules support the goals of being honest, respecting one another's wishes, helping around the house, and so on.

1. If I forget to clean up my things, I will have to:

_____

2. If I finish all my homework for this week, I will get to:

_____

3. _____

4. _____

5. _____

Now that is reasonable!

TAKE-HOME ACTIVITY

NAME: _____

ACTIVITY TWO: DON'T LAUGH, BE KIND!

Until people start making fun of King Bikhard's big teeth, he actually enjoys having them. He is able to chop down trees and scare away fierce animals. Below are six characters from the *1001 Nights* world. Each one has a feature or characteristic that they feel sensitive about. Can you help them figure out something positive about this feature or characteristic?

Oh, no! I have really huge ears.

I gave away my money to others, and now I have nothing. I'm not very smart.

Oh, no! I have a really big nose.

TAKE-HOME ACTIVITY

NAME: _____

GIVE UNTIL IT HURTS

Story Summary

At a county fair, Shahzaman gets annoyed at Donyazad for giving away their bag of pistachios to some hungry kids. Shahrzad tells Shahzaman the following story about charity and generosity:

Hassan, a simple and poor spice merchant from the city of Susa, inherits a fortune from a long-lost uncle and suddenly has a lot of "friends." Hassan is naively generous, and guided by his new "friends," he spends all his money on lavish dinners, new clothes, furniture, and parties for him and his friends. When Hassan's money runs out, he finds himself alone and broke on the street, so he turns to his friends, only to find that none will help him. As he despairs in the cold, a mysterious man appears and takes him to his mansion, where he is cleaned and fed. As Hassan laments his foolishness for giving everything away, the man tells Hassan he is still wealthy. As it turns out, the mysterious man is a beggar who Hassan gave money to as an act of generosity when he was rich. The beggar invested the money, started a business, and became very wealthy. Then the beggar tells Hassan he is giving him half of his fortune for his prior generosity. When Hassan thanks him in disbelief, the mystery man repeats the words Hassan said to him after giving him a bag of coins when he was a beggar: "If we don't help each other, then who will?" Shahzaman learns generosity has its own rewards.

Story Lessons
- Encourage children to be generous and to share with those who are less fortunate.
- Help children realize that although some people will take advantage of others' generosity, acts of kindness are still the right thing to do.
- Encourage children to understand that more fortunate people have a responsibility to help those less fortunate. Fulfilling this responsibility has its rewards for everyone.

CLASS PLAN

Pre-Viewing Activity (Approximately 5 Minutes)

Tell students a true story from your life about a time when a stranger did something kind for you. Maybe someone held the door when you were carrying a pile of books, or perhaps someone baked you a treat when you moved into the neighborhood. Maybe it was someone who offered you a compliment, a hug, or a smile. Invite students to share stories about a time when they did something kind or generous for another person. How did it make them feel?

Ask: What would you do if you suddenly found out you received a large amount of money from a long-lost relative you never knew? Would you keep it all or share some of it with other people? As they watch (or listen to) "Give Until It Hurts," they will see a man named Hassan face that very situation.

Watch or Read Episode (Approximately 10 Minutes)

Post-Viewing Discussion Questions (Approximately 10 Minutes)

Why did Hassan help the beggar? Did he expect anything in return? What did he mean when he said "If we don't help each other, then who will?"
(*Discussion:* Hassan helped the beggar because he believed that everyone has a responsibility to help those in need. He did not expect anything in return. When he said "If we don't help each other, then who will," he meant that if people don't show compassion for their fellow human beings in trouble, then these people will continue to suffer.)

What does Shahrzad mean when she says, "Generosity is its own reward"?
(*Discussion:* When we act kindly toward others, it often makes us feel better about ourselves, because we know we are making the world a better place. One shouldn't help others in order to get something in return, but rather, because it shows compassion toward other people and because those who have more should help those who have less.)

Why did many of Hassan's "friends" ignore him once he ran out of money? Why do you think they were nice to him when he was rich? Do you think they were really his friends or not?
(*Discussion:* Hassan's "friends" weren't really friends. They were just people taking advantage of Hassan's good luck. If they were really his friends, they would have shared their possessions with him, invited him into their homes, and so on.)

In-Class Activity – for 50-60 Minute Lessons (Approximately 30 Minutes)

It is very important to help others who are less fortunate. First, discuss organizations in society that help people in need. Then have the kids brainstorm ways they can do something to help such organizations. Then discuss who in society we consider to be people in need and what class members can do to help such people.

Write the following sentence on the board: "We act kindly toward other people because." Ask students to finish the sentence and write various responses on the board. Teachers should stress that they should not act kind because they expect something in return.

ACTIVITY ONE: SMALL ACTS OF KINDNESS

Some people think that being generous means giving away large sums of money. Not true! Little, low-cost actions can have a powerful impact—and can make you feel great. Here are some simple examples. Add your ideas to the list. Then for the next week, do an experiment. Every day, do at least one of the items from the list. In next week's class, we can discuss what you did and whether or not acting generous was a good experience. We've filled in the first entry to give you a simple example.

1. Help your family clean the house.

2.

3.

4.

5.

TAKE-HOME ACTIVITY

NAME: _____

ACTIVITY TWO: TRUE FRIENDS, FALSE FRIENDS.

LESSON SEVEN

In the episode, Hassan discovers the people he thought were his real friends (and whom he gave much of his money to) were false friends. They only cared about Hassan when he had something to give them.

Directions: With your family, talk about words that describe true friends (people who stick with you no matter what) and false friends (people who act friendly to you only when they can get something out of it, such as free food, clothing etc.). Would you prefer to be a true friend to someone else or a false friend? Under the pictures below, write characteristics of each.

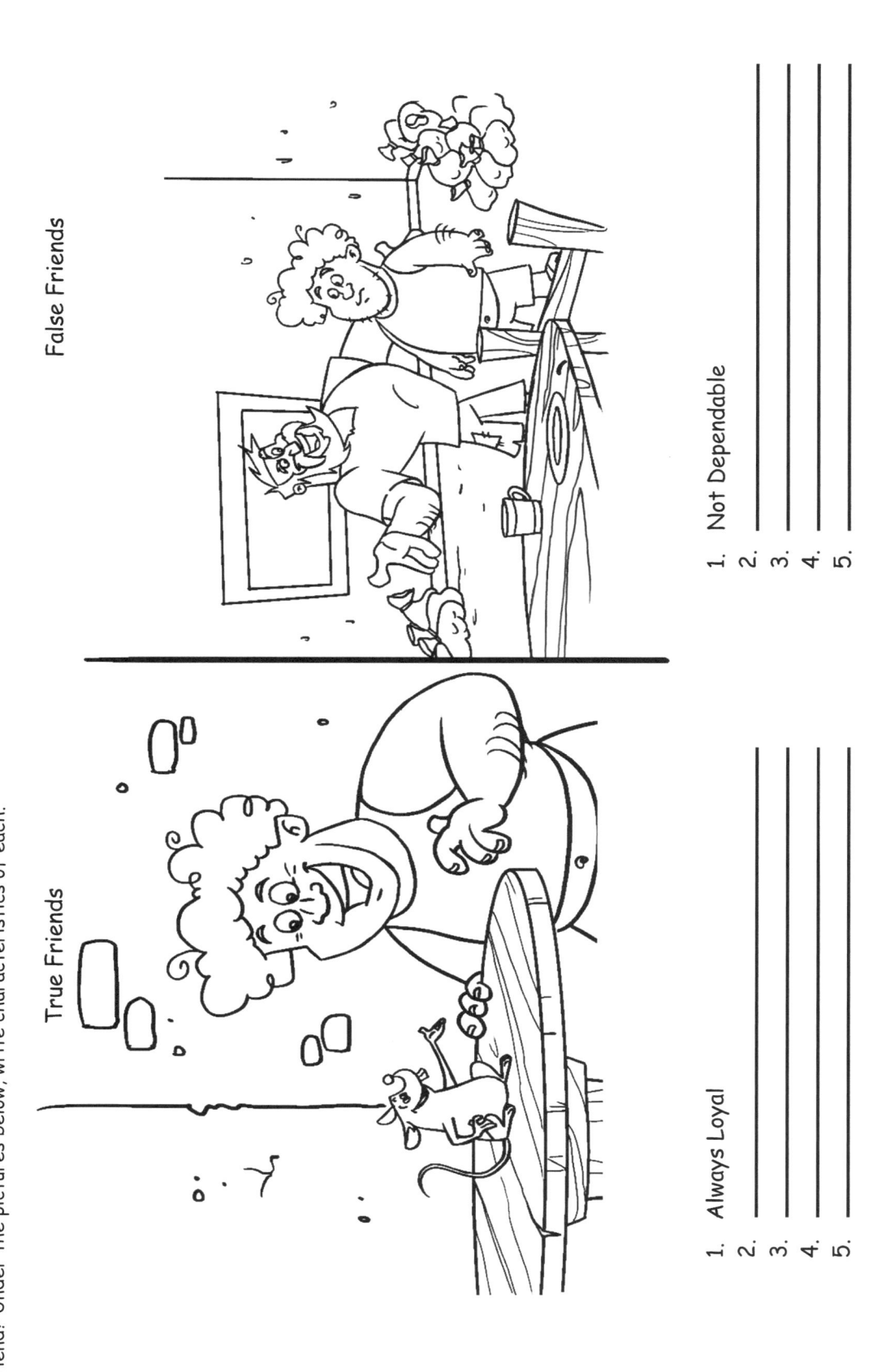

True Friends

False Friends

True Friends
1. Always Loyal
2. _____
3. _____
4. _____
5. _____

False Friends
1. Not Dependable
2. _____
3. _____
4. _____
5. _____

TAKE-HOME ACTIVITY

NAME: _____

HUNCHBACK'S TALE

Story Summary

When Shahryar can't find his favorite coat, he blames his servants and threatens to punish all of them if no one confesses. In the midst of his rampage, Shahrzad and the kids return from the tailor where, as it turns out, they took Shahryar's coat to have it fixed. Shahrzad then tells the embarrassed Shahryar that it's easy to jump to conclusions. Things aren't always what they seem to be. She tells him the story of the Hunchback:

Two men are tormenting a man named Ling, who happens to be a hunchback. When the emperor passes by, he takes pity on the man and brings him to the palace, where he orders his servants to treat him as his honored guest. Through a series of events, several people think they have accidentally killed Ling. Fearing the consequences, they all try to hide the body, in order not to be punished. When a sea captain is about to be punished, all the others confess, in order to prevent another person from being wrongfully found guilty. In the end, Ling pops back to life and everyone is relieved he is okay.

Story Lessons
- Help children understand it is sometimes easy to jump to conclusions. Remember that appearances can be deceiving.
- Encourage children to show compassion for individuals who are, in some way, different.
- Inspire children to admit when they have done something wrong, rather than try to cover up the evidence. Telling the truth is very important.
- Teach children that before you accuse someone of doing something wrong, you need to know the facts.

CLASS PLAN

Pre-Viewing Activity (Approximately 5 Minutes)

To help get students thinking about the idea that appearances can be deceiving, tell them to imagine this situation: you can't find your jacket at school. A week later, you see another student wearing that same jacket. What do you do? After students give their answers, reveal that the student happens to own the same style jacket in the same color. The next day, you discover your missing jacket at home. What do you do then? After a brief discussion, tell the students they are about to watch (or listen to) a story that deals with this subject.

Watch or Read Episode (Approximately 10 Minutes)

Post-Viewing Discussion Questions (Approximately 10 Minutes)

When you do something wrong or make a mistake, what is the best way to deal with the mistake? Why?
(*Discussion:* It is better to be honest and upfront. It's always easier to tell the truth; that way you have nothing to hide. Often when you tell lies, they force you to tell more lies, and the problem can get worse and worse. In contrast, when you are honest and admit mistakes, people are usually more understanding.)

Have you ever been accused of something you did not do? How did it make you feel? Have you ever accused someone of something they didn't do?
(*Discussion:* Discuss examples raised by the students and how it made them feel.)

What is the difference between doing something accidentally and intentionally? Do you think people should be punished for accidental mistakes?
(*Discussion:* No, unless they were doing something they were not supposed to be doing. If someone's actions lead to unintended consequences, then they should not be punished. Accidents happen; they are a part of life. We need to forgive and accept others' mistakes, if we want others to forgive and accept ours.)

In-Class Activity – for 50-60 Minute Lessons (Approximately 30 Minutes)

Ask students to raise their hands if they've ever made a mistake. Of course, all hands will go up. Yes, everyone makes mistakes. How do you feel when someone apologizes to you about making a mistake versus when they try to lie to you about it? Why? Generate a classroom discussion around the three following scenarios:

1. Person A is in a restaurant and gets up from their table to use the bathroom. Person B walks by Person A's table and bumps it, knocking over a glass of water, which spills on Person A's jacket. Person A comes back. What does Person B do? What should Person B do? Why?

2. A student has forgotten to do her homework. When she comes to school, her teacher asks everyone to hand in their assignments. What does the student say? Why? What should the student do?

3. Two teams are playing football, and Player A is offside, but scores a goal. Nobody notices. What does Player A do? What should Player A do? Why?

Have a discussion about which approach – the lying and deceitful vs. the honest and direct- was the smarter way to go. What happens when you lie? What happens when you tell the truth about something? How do people view you differently?

ACTIVITY ONE: MY FRIEND THE HUNCHBACK

LESSON EIGHT

When you meet someone different from you, it is easy to make judgments. It's much better, however, if you take the time to get to know people who are different and appreciate who they are as people, no matter how different they look, or are, from you. Here's your chance. Write a note to your parents about a new friend you just made when you took the time to get to know him or her.

I just made a great new friend. Other people call him the hunchback, because he has a curved back. But his real name is

_____, and we love to _____

TAKE-HOME ACTIVITY

NAME: _____

ACTIVITY TWO: TWO SIDES OF THE STORY

It's easy to jump to conclusions when you see something out of the ordinary. But before you accuse someone of something, you need to know the facts. Have a look at the two pictures below and tell us what seems to be happening, and then come up with an alternate explanation.

Hey! Are you stealing a cookie?

What SEEMS to be happening?:

What's REALLY going on:
(Hint: Shahzaman has a cloth in his hand.)

What SEEMS to be happening?:

What's REALLY going on:
(Hint: the kids are in math class, where Shahzaman struggles, but Donyazad does well.)

TAKE-HOME ACTIVITY

NAME: _____

ABU SABIR

Story Summary

When Donyazad throws a tantrum to get Shahryar to buy her a new cool pair of shoes that all the kids are wearing, Shahrzad tells her she doesn't need to follow what other kids do in order to be popular. To explain her point, she tells her the story of Abu Sabir:

Abu Sabir is a simple farmer. His wife, Bahar, longs to be part of the sophisticated elite who go to fancy dinner parties. She's jealous of her wealthy neighbors and gets angry that her husband appears to have no ambition. He's content being a simple, hardworking farmer. When the town learns of treasure hidden in a cave in the mountains, everyone heads up into the hills to get rich – everyone except Abu Sabir. He remains home to tend his crops, while his wife, Bahar, fumes in disbelief. The townspeople find the cave filled with treasure, but they get snowed in and have to wait for spring before they can return home. By that time, their crops are dead, their businesses abandoned, and their houses ruined. The only person with food and crops to sell is Abu Sabir. In need of provisions, the townspeople trade their newfound treasures for Abu Sabir's crops. He quickly becomes the richest man in town, but he continues to find happiness in simple pleasures. Bahar learns that integrity and hard work are the true measures of success, and simple pleasures can bring happiness.

Story Lessons
- Help children understand they don't need to do what is popular in order to be successful and happy.
- Encourage children to be grateful for the simple pleasures they already have.
- Help children learn that get-rich-quick schemes usually don't work. Worthwhile rewards mostly come from hard work, honesty, and patience.
- Encourage children not to be jealous of superficial successes and materialism and to look to integrity as a better route to happiness.

CLASS PLAN

Pre-Viewing Activity (Approximately 5 Minutes)

Hand out sheets of blank paper. Ask students to privately write down three reasons why someone might want to be friends with them. For example, they might write "I am very patient," "I can tell funny jokes," "I'm a fantastic listener," "I read a lot of books," or "I am good at making up games." Collect all the papers and then read aloud some of the student responses in random order. Write down a number of these qualities on the board. Choose a few of the qualities as examples and discuss: If you were going to make friends with someone, would you choose someone who's rich but mean, or someone who's nice (or has some of the good qualities listed on the board), even if he or she doesn't have a lot of money? Explain that, in this episode, Donyazad thinks that she will be more popular if she buys a pair of new shoes. Do you think this would make more people want to be friends with her?

Watch or Read Episode (Approximately 10 Minutes)

Post-Viewing Discussion Questions (Approximately 10 Minutes)

What are some ways to be a good friend?
(*Discussion:* Be a good listener, share your hobbies with others, be honest, and say something kind about the other person.)

Why was Abu Sabir so happy and satisfied, even before he became rich?
(*Discussion:* He is a patient, hardworking person who does not get caught up in superficial social pressures and trends. His honesty and integrity prevent him from discriminating against others.)

What is a get-rich-quick scheme? If a friend told you there was a hidden treasure in a nearby village, would you go? Why or why not?
(*Discussion:* A get-rich-quick-scheme is some offer that claims to give wonderful rewards for very little time or effort. If I heard about a hidden treasure, I might be tempted to go, but I would be very skeptical, because most get-rich-quick schemes are not worth it. Chances are, it would be a waste of time. Real rewards come from hard work, perseverance, being nice to others, and a little good luck.)

What is peer pressure? Why is it important to think for yourself?
(*Discussion:* Peer pressure is the act of doing something you know you shouldn't be doing, simply because others are doing it. It is important to think for yourself and make decisions based on your beliefs of what is right and wrong. Peer pressure can lead to bad decision making.)

In-Class Activity – for 50-60 Minute Lessons (Approximately 30 Minutes)

Explain to the students that peer pressure is a powerful thing because all children want to fit in. Standing up for the right thing takes courage.

Tell each student to pick two partners so that each student is in a group of three people. They will each take a turn playing the good person and resisting peer pressure in the following three scenarios. In each, the good person needs to try to convince the other two that they should not break the rules.

Here are the scenarios:

1. Two of the students want to sneak away from school during the day
2. There are three problems in a homework assignment. Two of the students come up with the idea that they should each do one problem and copy each other's answers.
3. Two students want to play a practical joke on another student in a way that may make the other student feel embarrassed or hurt.

Afterward, the whole class talks about the power of peer pressure. Discuss each of the following scenarios and discuss different reasons why the good person refused to follow the other two. Was it hard for the good person to challenge the others? Why?

ACTIVITY ONE: BECOME A FRIEND MAGNET

Making friends can be challenging, but the rewards are worth it. Sometimes we forget that the best way to make a new friend is to act like the kind of person you'd want to befriend.

I wish I had more friends. What should I do?

How to Make More Friends

Talk to your family to come up with five things Donyazad can do to make more friends.

1. _____

2. _____

3. _____

4. _____

5. _____

TAKE-HOME ACTIVITY

NAME: _____

ACTIVITY TWO: ABU SABIR'S SECRET TO HAPPINESS

Directions: Make a list of five activities that don't cost money but always boost your mood. Put this list on a wall so you can remember what to do the next time you feel sad.

My secret to happiness is that I work the fields, and they grow into hearty crops. I also love to sing, read, and play with my donkey.

I don't get it. You have very little money. You don't have any fancy clothes. You live in a simple house. **Why are you so happy?**

What are some things that make YOU happy?

1. _____

2. _____

3. _____

4. _____

5. _____

TAKE-HOME ACTIVITY

NAME: _____

SINBAD AND THE VALLEY OF SERPENTS

Story Summary

A poor porter named Sinbad hates his job and wishes he could have a better life. Shahrzad insists he can change his life, and then tells him the story of another man named Sinbad who started out poor but and ended up rich:

Sinbad sails the seas with his trusty sidekicks, Dina and Peta (a monkey), as they seek out adventure and riches. They discover an island, only to find it's actually the back of a sea monster that swallows them up. Thankfully, Dina figures out how to get out of the beast's belly. They wind up on a deserted island and, due to Sinbad's greed and poor judgment, come face-to-face with death by angering monster-size serpents and rukh birds. Luckily, Dina saves them, proving she is the true brains of the team. Eventually, they escape with the jewels in hand.

Though fraught with personal limitations, Sinbad is an ordinary man who changed his destiny through hard work and creativity. If Sinbad can succeed through hard work, everyone can.

Story Lessons
- Help children understand they have the power to change their lives through hard work and perseverance.
- Inspire children to believe in their ability to control their own destinies.

CLASS PLAN

Pre-Viewing Activity (Approximately 5 Minutes)

Ask students: What do you want to be when you grow up? The children can suggest different professions or different people they would like to be. The teacher should write their suggestions on the board. If the children struggle to come up with professions, the teacher should help list different ones.

Discuss different careers that are listed and explain that any career goal takes time, planning, and persistence. Discuss how some of the goals on the board might be achieved. What are some steps that students could take now to find out more about these careers?

Explain that some goals are big (like preparing to become a teacher or an astronaut) – whereas others are small (like preparing for a test the next week or learning to ride a bicycle).

Introduce the episode by saying they will meet two men, both named Sinbad, who have BIG goals about making their lives better.

Watch or Read Episode (Approximately 10 Minutes)

Post-Viewing Discussion Questions (Approximately 10 Minutes)

Shahrzad insists that Sinbad the porter can make his life better. Do you believe people can improve their lives? Why or why not?
(*Discussion:* People can improve their lives, if they work hard.)

In real life, you can't just make your life better by making a wish. If you really want to make your life better, what are some of the things you need to do?
(*Discussion:* Review the process of setting clear, realistic goals, breaking down large goals into smaller steps, working hard, and not giving up when you encounter setbacks.)

What would have happened to Sinbad if he had given up when his plans failed?
(*Discussion:* If Sinbad had not persisted when he encountered failure, then he would have never discovered the riches he found with his team.)

In-Class Activity – for 50-60 Minute Lessons
(Approximately 30 Minutes)

Have the teacher mediate a discussion where the children discuss different professions and why they are good (or not so good) as things to strive to become. Here, the teacher can go back to the list of professions they created earlier. Have the teacher pick two of them (say, a doctor and a pilot) and lead a discussion where the kids suggest different things they would need to do in order to become a doctor or a pilot.

ACTIVITY ONE: WHAT DO YOU WANT TO BE WHEN YOU GROW UP?

Achieving a big goal can feel like magic! But reaching a big goal can take lots of hard work and not giving up when you have setbacks.

Directions: Pick a career you might like to have when you grow up and then list the different steps you need to achieve this goal. Here are some careers you might consider: teacher, doctor, lawyer, scientist, businessperson, journalist, governor, president, police officer, chef/cook.

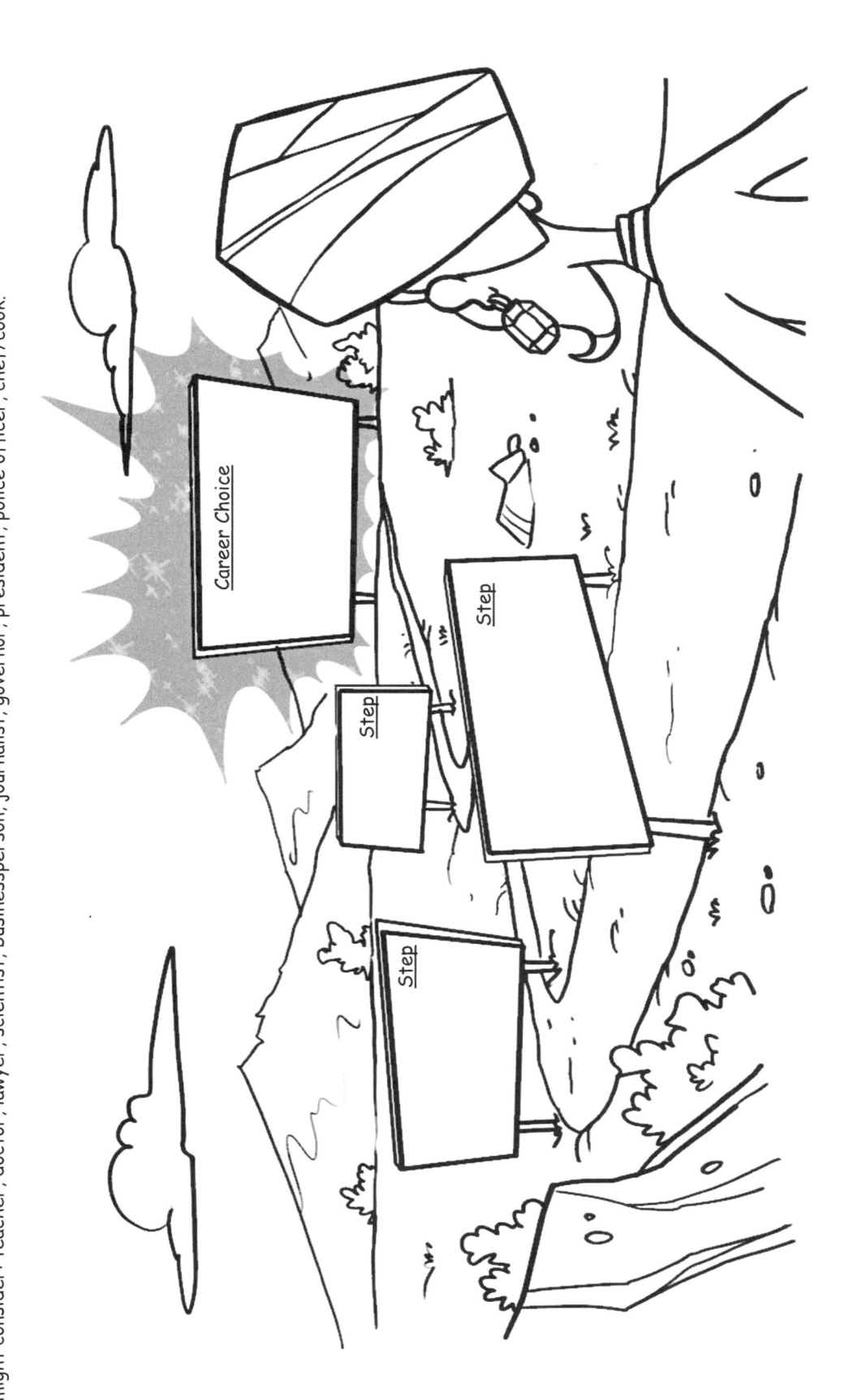

Career Choice

Step

Step

Step

TAKE-HOME ACTIVITY

NAME: _____

ACTIVITY TWO: WHAT DO YOU WANT? HOW DO YOU GET THERE?   LLESSON TEN

Directions: Work with a grownup in your family to identify three goals that you'd like to achieve – one by the end of today, one by the end of this month, and one by the end of this year. Smaller goals can be achieved in a day. Others require many months of hard work. The more clear and more specific you make goals and the steps to achieve them, the better your chances of achieving them.

BY THE END OF TODAY	BY THE END OF THIS MONTH	BY THE END OF THE YEAR
Goal: Steps Needed to Achieve It: Possible Obstacles: Is It Realistic?	Goal: Steps Needed to Achieve It: Possible Obstacles: Is It Realistic?	Goal: Steps Needed to Achieve It: Possible Obstacles: Is It Realistic?

TAKE-HOME ACTIVITY   NAME: _____

DETAILS, DETAILS

Story Summary

When Shahzaman doesn't bother to number the pages on his homework, Shahrzad reminds him that attention to detail can make a big difference. She tells him the following story:

A man repairing the wheel on a carriage doesn't bother to tighten the nut properly. As a result, the wheel falls off on its next trip, which causes a cook to miss a boat upon which he is scheduled to work. When the ship leaves without its cook, and someone with no experience does the cooking, the crew gets food poisoning and can't sail properly. Eventually, the ship crashes and sinks. All the cargo is lost, including some empty cans that are used to hold glue. The factory that ships the glue now has to use oil bottles instead of glue cans to ship their glue. The oil bottles, which are now filled with glue, are delivered to the wheelhouse of a dam. The two men manning the dam think they are putting oil on the wheel of a floodgate to make it move better, but instead of oil, they use glue on the dam hinges. The floodgate is now glued shut, so the dam overflows and destroys an entire town below. All learn a lesson in the importance of tiny details, because one man did not properly tighten the nut on a wheel, an entire town was destroyed.

Story Lessons
- Help children appreciate that small details can sometimes make a big difference down the line. Do the best you can, or others could be harmed.
- Remind children that their actions often affect more than themselves.
- Teach children the importance of diligence and attention to detail in their work.

CLASS PLAN

Pre-Viewing Activity (Approximately 5 Minutes)

Ask the class to brainstorm and then discuss the simple steps that one goes through to accomplish an everyday task. List the basic steps on the board and try to be as correct as possible. Discuss what would happen if the order was accidentally not followed correctly or if a step was missed. As an example, the activity could be taking a shower. A mistake would be getting under the water before taking off your clothes. Use this example as a method of explaining why being detail oriented and paying attention is very important.

Watch or Read Episode (Approximately 10 Minutes)

Post-Viewing Discussion Questions (Approximately 10 Minutes)

How might things have turned out differently if the wagon's nut had been properly tightened at the start?
(*Discussion:* If the man had taken the time to properly tighten the nut, the wagon would not have broken down, and the chef would have made it onboard the ship. The ship would have had a cook, so all the crew would be okay and the ship would not have sunk. The ship, therefore, would have delivered the glue cans, and the men in the factory would not have put glue in the oil cans. As a result, the two men in the wheelhouse would not have put glue on the dam hinge, and the hinge would have been able to open to protect the town.)

Why is it sometimes easy to overlook small details?
(*Discussion:* People mistakenly think small details are not important, so they ignore them. They forget that small details are often connected to other small details, which can have a big impact.)

What did you learn from this story?
(*Discussion:* It is important to make sure you do your work thoroughly. If you are not careful, other people can suffer. Society is very interconnected.)

Do you think Shahzaman will number the pages of his homework the next time? Why or why not?
(*Discussion:* Shahzaman will probably number his pages, because he learned why this detail is important. The page numbers make it easier to reorder the pages if they accidentally get mixed up.)

In-Class Activity – for 50-60 Minute Lessons (Approximately 30 Minutes)

To learn the importance of small details, the class plans a mock party. As a group, the class determines the purpose of the party (such as to celebrate the birthday of the school founder, a national hero, or an author). The class decides the major steps required to plan the party and then is divided into small groups of two or three students (one group handles decorations, another is responsible for refreshments, etc.). Each group then writes a very detailed list of everything they need to do to accomplish their portion of the party. Each small group then presents their plan to the class, and the class helps them think of what details they may have overlooked. The teacher can spark critical thinking by asking questions of each small group: What would happen if the group bought cups that were too big? What if you forgot to tell people the time of the event? You didn't mention tape. How are you going to attach the posters to the wall?

ACTIVITY ONE: WHO ELSE COULD HAVE SAVED THE DAM?

This story showed that a tiny detail – a man not tightening a nut on a wagon wheel – could lead to multiple negative consequences. But the problem of the dam overflowing could have been prevented if other people in the town had been more careful and diligent.

Directions: Write down a response to each person's statement on how they could have done things differently.

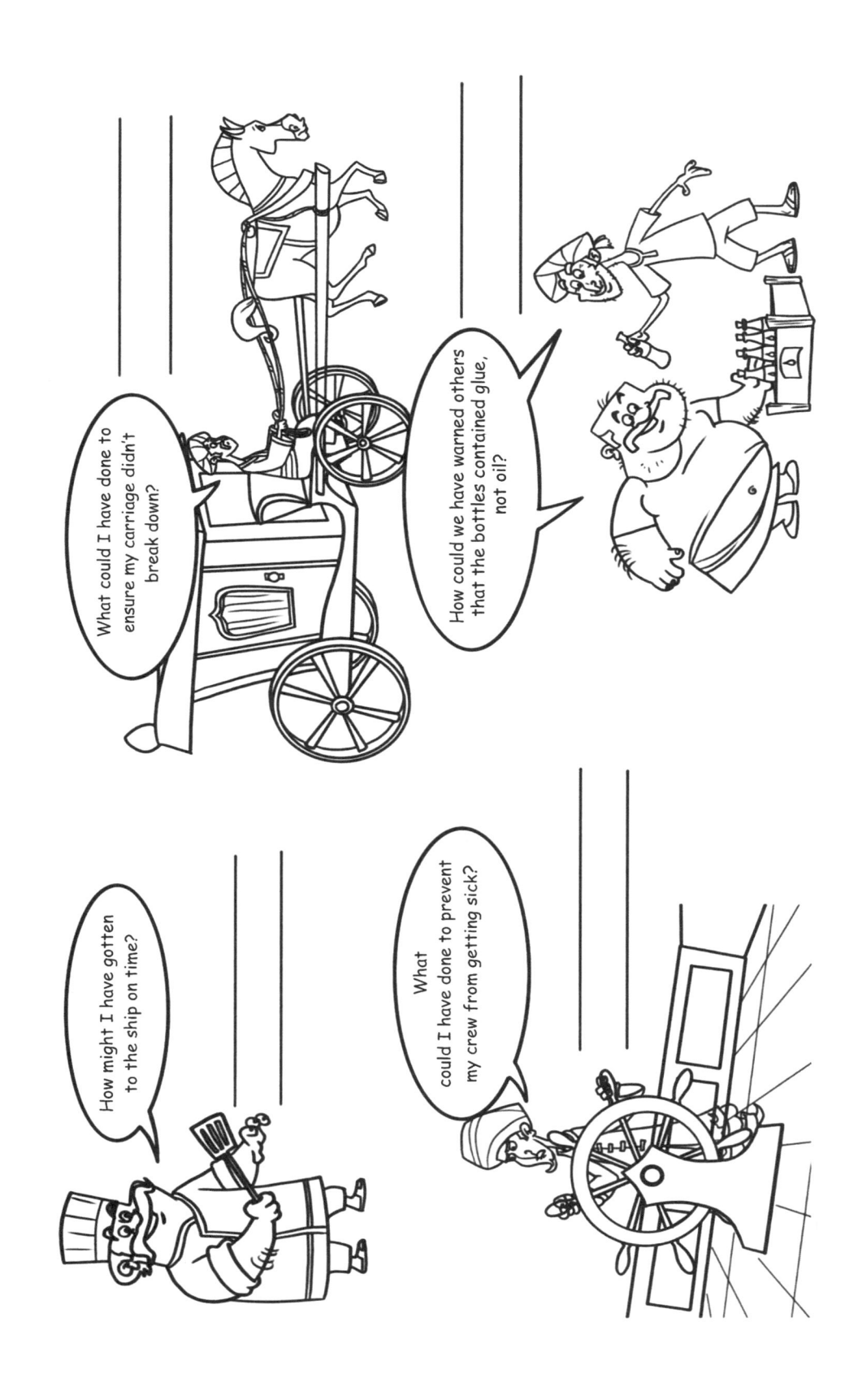

What could I have done to ensure my carriage didn't break down?

How could we have warned others that the bottles contained glue, not oil?

How might I have gotten to the ship on time?

What could I have done to prevent my crew from getting sick?

TAKE-HOME ACTIVITY

NAME: _____

ACTIVITY TWO: CAUSE AND EFFECT

In our story, a man forgot to tighten a screw and as a result an entire village was destroyed. Now it's your turn to use your imagination to tell a story with a big conclusion, starting with how you woke up tired and did not tie your laces properly.

On Saturday, I was really tired,	so I did not tie my shoe laces properly,	and as a result _____ _____
_____ _____ _____ _____	_____ _____ _____ _____	_____ _____ _____ _____
_____ _____ _____	_____ _____ _____	_____ _____ _____

NAME: _____

MANJAB'S JUST DESSERTS

Story Summary

While Chef Rajani is out of the kitchen, Donyazad and Shahzaman sneak a piece of his freshly baked cake, only to end up eating the entire thing. When Chef Rajani loses his cool, Shahrzad tells the kids about a boy who stole food and got just what he deserved:

Manjab was an honest, hardworking boy who worked in a bakery. When he accidentally ruins a pie, Ravi, his pet cockatoo, suggests they eat it instead of telling the owner. At first, Manjab considers this to be stealing, but he allows himself to be persuaded. Both he and Ravi gobble down the pie. When they get away with it, Manjab realizes that stealing is easy and very delicious. Soon, he and Ravi begin sneaking more treats and covering up their tracks so that the owner is unaware. It all goes well for Manjab until he starts to put on weight. Before he knows it, his thievery becomes as plain as the rolls of fat on his body. In the end, Manjab gets his just desserts when he learns that stealing is wrong, and he suffers the consequences of gluttony.

Story Lessons
- Help children understand that stealing is wrong morally, whether you are caught or not.
- Teach children that you may get away with stealing once or twice, but eventually, stealing and lying catch up to you, and you will be caught.
- Encourage children to resist peer pressure when someone tries to tempt them to do the wrong thing.
- Encourage children to eat a healthy diet and not overindulge in sweets.
- Help children understand that admitting they have made a mistake and dealing with the consequences is much better than trying to cover it up with a lie.

CLASS PLAN

Pre-Viewing Activity (Approximately 5 Minutes)

Tell students to imagine that they came home after school and discovered a big plate of sweets like baklava on the kitchen table. Describe the sweets in mouth-watering detail. Mention that there is no one else in the kitchen and you don't know whose sweets they are. First ask them: Would it be okay to eat just one? Then ask: What about if you returned home with some friends? Would it be okay for each of you to eat one of the treats? Then ask: What if you went to a friend's house and saw the sweets in their kitchen. Is it okay to take just one without permission? Finally ask: What if you are in a bakery, and the baker left some of his cookies out to cool. Would it be okay to have one?

Have a summarizing discussion and ask whether the circumstances make one action worse than the other. Make it clear that taking anything that is not yours, without permission is wrong - it violates trust and is stealing.

Watch or Read Episode (Approximately 10 Minutes)

Post-Viewing Discussion Questions (Approximately 10 Minutes)

What was the first thing Manjab stole? Was the first treat he stole big or little? Do you think Manjab would have taken anything if Ravi first told him, "Let's take everything in the store"? Why or why not?
(*Discussion:* First, Manjab was persuaded by his friend Ravi to take "just one" treat. Taking one item didn't seem so bad to Manjab, but after he stole it, he started to think that stealing more things wouldn't be too bad either – until he stole almost everything in the bakery.)

What are some good ways to say no to a friend who tries to persuade you to lie, steal, or do something wrong?
(*Discussion:* You can tell the friend that stealing and lying are wrong, and you don't want to do it. You can say you don't want to get into trouble.)

At one point, Manjab and Ravi decide to "destroy the evidence" by eating the cake they damaged. What should they have done instead?
(*Discussion:* Manjab and Ravi could have told the baker the truth, apologized, and offered to pay for a new cake or to help in his shop. The baker probably would have been forgiving if they told the truth. By lying, they made the situation worse.)

In-Class Activity – for 50-60 Minute Lessons (Approximately 30 Minutes)

Activity: Tell the students that you are going to pretend to be a "superbad person" who makes bad decisions and usually gets into trouble. Invite a series of volunteers to come before the class and attempt to persuade them to do something wrong. Ask the volunteer and then the class how they should respond and why? Some sample situations are:

1. Look at this wall - wouldn't it be fun to write something funny on it? No one is looking!
2. Pretend we're in a store. Oh, doesn't that candy look delicious? Who cares if you don't have enough money to buy it? Take one. They have lots of candy! No one will notice!
3. Let's not do our homework. We can go out and play and just say we didn't do our homework because we were sick!
4. So you forgot your pens and books at home? I think there are some in the teacher's supply room. You can sneak in and take some. It's no big deal, it's for school!
5. There's that guy with the funny hair. Let's go make fun of him and make him cry!

ACTIVITY ONE: HEALTHY CHOICES

To do well in school, and live a long life, you need to eat a variety of healthy foods. Some sugary treats are okay once in a while, but if you eat too much of them, you'll end up with bad teeth and poor health.

Circle the foods you think will help make your muscles strong and your mind alert. Then talk about your choices with a family member. Then work with a family member to create a healthy menu for one day.

Use this space to create a healthy Menu for one day.

Breakfast:

_____

_____

Lunch:

_____

_____

Dinner:

_____

_____

Snacks during the day:

_____

TAKE-HOME ACTIVITY

NAME: _____

ACTIVITY TWO: HELP MANJAB RESIST RAVI'S URGING!

LESSON TWELVE

In this episode, Munjab and Ravi act in horrible ways: they steal, they lie, and they overeat. Manjab needs your help to live a more honest life.

In the picture below, Munjab and Ravi are left alone in a candy store because the store owner went to buy some tea. Before leaving the store owner asked Munjab if he could to mind the store for five minutes. Ravi is excited and drooling at the sweet delights that fill the shelves of the store.

Using the space on the right side of the page, work with your parents to write what Munjab's should tell to Ravi.

Use this space to write what Munjab should tell Ravi

Ravi! NO!

Can you believe it? It's all ours for the taking! Oooh, lollipops, my favorite!

TAKE-HOME ACTIVITY

NAME: _____

ALI BABA AND THE FORTY THIEVES

Note: Prior to class, teacher's leading a one-hour class should make multiple copies of Activity Sheet Two.

Story Summary

When Shahzaman accuses Donyazad of stealing his bag of sweets, Shahrzad notices their monkey, Maymoon, has a guilty look on his face. She tells them this story:

Ali Baba, an honest and hardworking boy, awakes one morning to find that Tabnak and his gang of forty thieves has robbed every home in his poor village. Ali Baba locates Tabnak's secret cave in the mountains and brings the stolen property back to his village. Furious, Tabnak and his forty thieves return that night and steal back everything, including two jars in which Ali Baba and Marjaneh are hiding. The thieves carry the jars into the cave without realizing that Ali Baba and Marjaneh are inside. The two outwit Tabnak and his men, and then the townspeople arrive and arrest the thieves. In the end, Tabnak learns that the only way for a thief to make amends is to give back everything he stole. He is forced to go from home to home and return everything he stole.

Story Lessons
- Help children learn that stealing is wrong, because it hurts other people. Stealing robs people of more than just property. It also takes away feelings of trust in others.
- Teach children that if someone does steal, the only way for him or her to make things right is to return what was stolen and then apologize.
- Encourage children to empathize with people who are robbed.

CLASS PLAN

Pre-Viewing Activity (Approximately 5 Minutes)

Ask students to think of a special item they own that they would miss if it were suddenly gone. Encourage them to include objects that have sentimental as well as monetary value, such as a photograph of a relative—things that are truly irreplaceable. Have four or five volunteers tell the class what their special items are. Discuss what it would feel like if these objects were stolen. How would it feel if the stolen items were then returned?

Watch or Read Episode (Approximately 10 Minutes)

Post-Viewing Discussion Questions (Approximately 10 Minutes)

Is stealing something small (say a bag of candy) different from stealing something big (say, a car)?
(*Discussion:* No, stealing is stealing. Taking things from others, no matter the monetary value, is mean and disrespectful.)

What are some consequences of stealing?
(*Discussion:* If you steal something, there is a high likelihood you will steal again. Once they start to steal, most thieves cannot stop. It is highly likely you will eventually be caught, but whether you are caught or not, you will live a life of insecurity and fear (of getting caught). You will also live a life absent of trust. And if the theft is big enough, you could even end up in jail.)

At the end of the episode, Shahzaman was disappointed in Maymoon. Why? What did he tell Maymoon to do? Was Shahzaman more upset about the sweets or about something being stolen by a friend?
(*Discussion:* Shazaman was surprised because Maymoon is his friend and pet monkey. Stealing is not just about taking things; it violates trust. Shahzaman told Maymoon he should have just asked for the sweets. If Maymoon had asked for the sweets, Shahzaman would have given them to him. Shahzaman did not care as much about the sweets, but did not like having someone take them from him, especially a friend.)

In-Class Activity – for 50-60 Minute Lessons (Approximately 30 Minutes)

For this activity, the teacher will photocopy and distribute copies of Activity Sheet Two. The teacher should go through each different scene. First, the kids should provide, by a show of hands, whether they think the situation equals theft. Then the class should have an open discussion on the ethics of the situation. Finally, whether the kids determine the scene to be theft or not, they should discuss what they should do in this situation.

ACTIVITY ONE: SWEET TREATS

In this story, Maymoon desperately wants to eat some sweets. In this exercise, help Maymoon get what he wants, the right way.

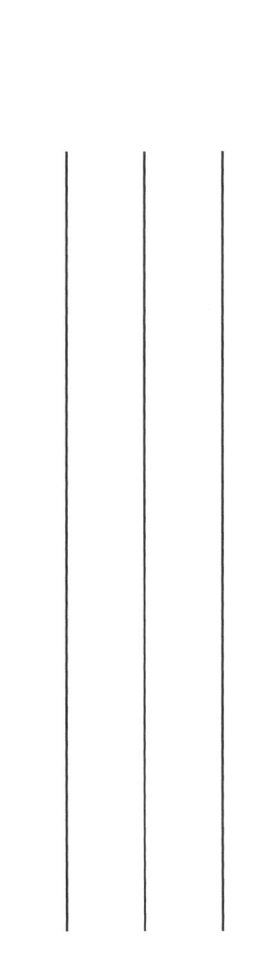

1. What are all the different ways Maymoon might get the sweets?

_____

_____

_____

_____

_____

2. Which might get Maymoon in trouble?

_____

_____

3. Which ways could get Maymoon the treats without getting in trouble?

_____

_____

_____

TAKE-HOME ACTIVITY

NAME: _____

ACTIVITY TWO: IS IT STEALING OR NOT

In this episode, Tabnak and his thieves take all sorts of things from others. While most people know that it is wrong to take something very valuable, like a gold ring, they sometimes are unclear about taking less valuable items. Talk about these situations with your family and decide, "Is it stealing or not?"

You find a bicycle on the street. You ride away on it. DO YOU THINK THIS IS STEALING? What should you do? _____

You copy the answers to a homework assignment, so you can go out and play. You say, "I knew all that stuff anyway." DO YOU THINK THIS IS STEALING?

You take an older-looking apple from a fruit stand. DO YOU THINK THIS IS STEALING?

You discover a wallet with money in a trash bin. You decide to take it. DO YOU THINK THIS IS STEALING? What should you do?

You borrow a pencil from a friend's desk without asking first. Do YOU THINK THIS IS STEALING? _____

ONE-HOUR CLASS - IN-CLASS ACTIVITY
HALF-HOUR CLASS - TAKE-HOME ACTIVITY

NAME: _____

PRINCE AHMAD

Story Summary

When Shahzaman is afraid to jump from the high dive, Maziar makes fun of him for being a coward. Shahrzad explains that common sense should never be confused with cowardice. She tells them the story of Prince Ahmad:

King Rishad has three sons, one of which will be the new king someday. Rishad puts each of them to the test, to see who is most fit to assume the throne. His eldest son, Husayn, is sent on a mission to negotiate fishing rights with a neighboring kingdom. When negotiations falter, Husayn refuses to back down or to show weakness. He declares war! Ali, the middle son, then plans a brilliant strategy to mobilize their forces and to surround the enemy. It is now left up to Prince Ahmad to lead the attack. After some soul-searching, Ahmad backs down and decides he won't take his country into war over something as trivial as fishing rights. At first, he is ashamed of his actions, calling them weak. His brothers are aghast, but his father intercedes, telling them all that Ahmad's unwillingness to make people fight and die over something as silly as fishing rights proves that he's not weak. King Rishad concludes that Prince Ahmad's decision to back out of a conflict and not fight was an act of courage.

Story Lessons
- Help children understand that refusing to fight is not an act of cowardice. In fact, such an approach is an act of intelligence and bravery.
- Inspire children to seek positive, nonviolent actions to resolve conflicts at home and in school.
- Encourage children to do the right thing, regardless of what others might think.

CLASS PLAN

Pre-Viewing Activity (Approximately 5 Minutes)

Write the following on the board: "chicken," "scaredy-cat," "coward," "baby," "weakling," and so on. Ask students how they would feel if someone called them one of these names. Would they be angry? Would they feel the urge to show they were brave and tough? Point out that no one likes to be called names. Tell the students that they are about to see (or hear) a story about a prince who learns there are different ways to respond to such names.

Watch or Read Episode (Approximately 10 Minutes)

Post-Viewing Discussion Questions (Approximately 10 Minutes)

Why did Prince Ahmad's brothers want to start a war? Do you think they were right or wrong? Why?
(*Discussion:* They thought starting a war would make them look strong. But they were wrong, because it's foolish to fight over something silly that doesn't really matter. If you're a king, it's even worse, because it means many people will die in a war.)

Why did Prince Ahmad decide not to go to war? Do you think he was right or wrong? Why?
(*Discussion:* Prince Ahmad did not want people to die, just so he could look brave. After listening to the people in town, he realized the people did not want to go to war and did not care about fishing rights. He cared more about his people than himself and decided that it would be better for people to think he was weak than to risk the lives of his people.)

Prince Ahmad worried that stopping the war would make people think he was weak. Do you think Prince Ahmad's decision was brave or weak? Why?
(*Discussion:* At first, Prince Ahmad believed that a brave person's only response to a conflict is to go on the attack. But he showed true bravery by saving people's lives, even if others might think he was weak for making that decision.)

What qualities do you think makes a person brave?
(*Discussion:* A brave person can be afraid of scary situations, but he or she takes the right action despite those fears. A brave person has the courage to stand up to others who say he or she is weak, if it means doing the right thing.)

In-Class Activity – for 50-60 Minute Lessons (Approximately 30 Minutes)

Give the class three examples of conflicts from the daily lives of children, and then have the class discuss how Prince Ahmad might have approached the problem.

1. A football team loses a game, and two people blame their teammate for missing a goal.
2. Two students want to take the same book from the library.
3. One child accidentally trips another, causing him or her to fall.
4. One child says something mean about another's drawing.
5. Two brothers are watching television, and each wants to watch something different.

Directions: Talk to your family about ways you can avoid fighting at home and at school. List some of them here (we've helped you with the first one).

1. Take a step back and take time to calm down.

2. _____

3. _____

4. _____

5. _____

Brother Ahmad has taught us that avoiding fights is a way of being strong.

TAKE-HOME ACTIVITY   NAME: _____

ACTIVITY TWO: WHY FIGHTING IS BAD

LESSON FOURTEEN

After I found a non violent way of stopping the conflict my brothers started, I decided to write a book. I wanted to tell all the people in my kingdom that not fighting can be courageous too.

Can you write the first page for me and explain why fighting should be avoided?

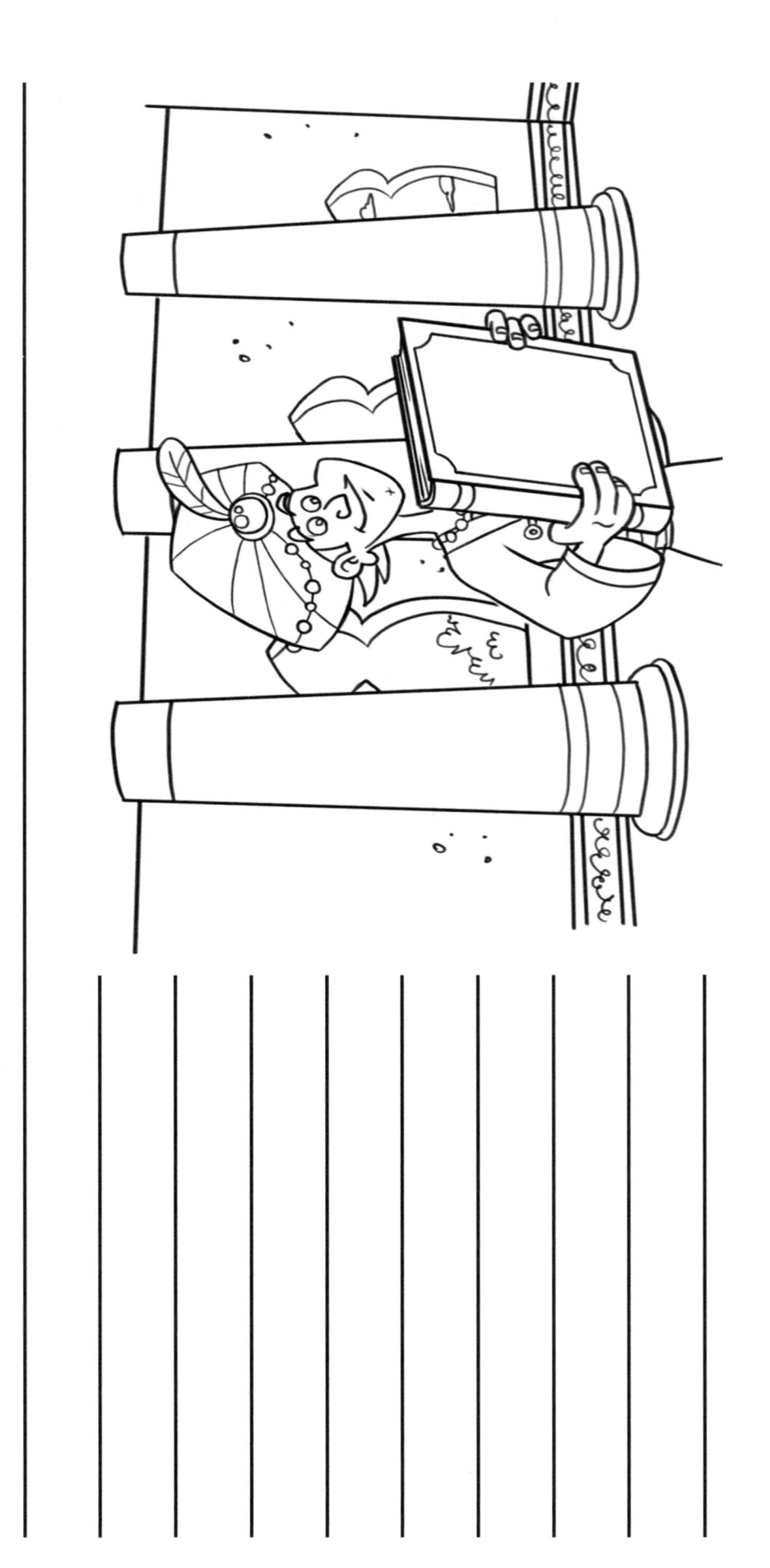

TAKE-HOME ACTIVITY

NAME: _____

IT'S A STEAL

Note: Prior to class, teachers will need to make multiple copies of Activity Sheet Two. This sheet should be cut in half so each student has an image of a happy Bromar or a grumpy Bromar for the pre-viewing exercise.

Story Summary

Shahryar slips on some marbles and blames Shahzaman for leaving them on the floor. Shahzaman says he didn't do it, but Shahryar insists the marbles belong to him. Shahzaman seems guilty. Shahrzad reminds Shahryar that things are sometimes not what they seem, and she tells him this story:

Several homes in a small town have been robbed. Everyone wonders who the thief could be. When two kids see their next-door neighbor, Bromar, return home late at night carrying a sack, they tell their parents, and the police go to Bromar's house. While Bromar denies any wrongdoing, they find stolen merchandise in his closet and arrest him. Bromar has always kept to himself, so people don't like him and immediately assume he is guilty. While Bromar is at the police station, the children figure out that it was Bromar's pet monkey, not Bromar, who was taking things from the homes. They also discover that Bromar is hard of hearing, which explains why he didn't talk with his neighbors very much and sometimes appeared rude. When the kids reveal the truth to the judge, everyone is ashamed that they allowed their prejudices to cloud their judgment, and every person should be presumed innocent until they are proven guilty. Bromar is set free, and embraced by the community.

Story Lessons

- Help children learn that appearances can be deceiving. Just because someone appears guilty does not mean that they committed a crime. One must carefully look at all the facts.
- Encourage children to give people the benefit of the doubt. There is often more than one explanation for a person's behavior.

CLASS PLAN

Pre-Viewing Activity (Approximately 5 Minutes)

Before class: Photocopy the two contrasting pictures of Bromar: one shows him smiling and friendly, the other shows him scowling and frowning. Cut these in half and give each student either a happy or grumpy version of Bromar.

Ask students to look at their pictures and have each of them privately write down five adjectives to describe this person. Ask them to decide if he is smart or not. Does this person have lots of friends? Is he nice? Approachable? Do you think he is an honest person? After students have had a chance to write their answers, tell them that you handed out two images of the same character and show them both images. Ask them to tell the class what adjectives they used and write two lists on the board, one for happy Bromar and one for grumpy Bromar. Now tell them that they are about to watch a video (or listen to a story) that will tell them more about this person.

Watch or Read Episode (Approximately 10 Minutes)

Post-Viewing Discussion Questions (Approximately 10 Minutes)

Why do Ava and Arsha avoid Bromar at first? What makes them realize their first impressions were wrong? How did your first impressions of Bromar influence your assumption of his character?
(*Discussion:* Bromar generally doesn't talk to other people, so Ava and Arsha's father assumes he's not a nice person. They change their opinion when they learn that Bromar's lack of communication is due to his having difficulty hearing. Our answers also showed that, based only on a picture, we were willing to make assumptions about who he was.)

How did the children solve the mystery of how all those possessions ended up in Bromar's house?
(*Discussion:* To figure out who really committed the crime, the children needed to review all the facts, ask lots of questions, and consider all the clues. Once they knew that Bromar was a nice, honest person, they had to look for another explanation for how the items got there. They realized that Bromar's monkey had accidentally broken into people's homes, taken some of their possessions, and put them in Bromar's closet.)

What would you do if someone accused you of something you didn't do?
(*Discussion:* I would calmly explain that his or her conclusion about the crime was wrong. I would offer an alternate explanation, so that the others would understand what really happened.)

If you thought someone did something wrong, what would you do?
(*Discussion:* Check it out, get all the facts, don't jump to conclusions, etc.)

In-Class Activity – for 50-60 Minute Lessons (Approximately 30 Minutes)

Explain (or ask for two student volunteers to act out) the following short scene. In the scene, a child notices a toy on the sidewalk and walks closer to look at it. The child recognizes the toy as something that belongs to his or her brother or sister. Suddenly, a second child walks right up to the toy, picks it up, and runs away.
Ask the class: What just happened? Some students will say that the second child stole the toy and ran off with it. Ask the class to think of alternate explanations. If they can't think of any, suggest that perhaps the toy on the ground looked similar to the toy the first kid recognized, and maybe it really belonged to the child who picked it up. What else? Maybe the child who found the toy picked it up because they wanted to find its rightful owner.

Talk about why it is important to gather all facts, and think about all the possibilities, before making a conclusion.

Explain (or ask for student volunteers to act out these scenes). After each one, invite the class to suggest all the possible explanations for what they observed.

At a playground, one child calls out to another, "Want to play?" But the second child doesn't even turn around.
o What do you think? What else could be going on?
o After the discussion, tell the class that the second child is deaf. It was not rudeness; after all, he or she didn't hear the request to play.

Your bicycle is missing and you see another boy riding your bicycle.
o What's going on? What do you do? What else could be going on?
o After the discussion, tell the class that the boy has the same bicycle as you and that was his bicycle, it just looked like yours.

You're on a train or bus, and another kid is sitting across from you. When you say hi to him, he looks at you and says nothing. Then when you tell him your name, he looks at you funny and then turns away to ignore you.
o What's going on and what do you think? What else could be going on?
o After a discussion, you tell the class that you then see him turn to his parents and hear him speak a different language. Now you realize he didn't understand what you were saying.

You're on the playground, and you turn around to see someone sitting in the corner, going through your bag.
o What do you think and what do you do? What else could be going on?
o You then tell the class that this person saw your backpack, but they didn't know whose backpack it was, so they were looking for information in the bag to find its rightful owner.

ACTIVITY ONE: DIG UP THE FACTS

When solving a mystery, it's important to look at all the available information and think very carefully before making a final decision.

Imagine you are missing something special - a toy, book, keys, or whatever. Where did it go? Try not to jump to conclusions. Collect all the facts you can and see if you can figure out the truth about what really happened. What questions should you ask yourself when trying to figure out what happened?

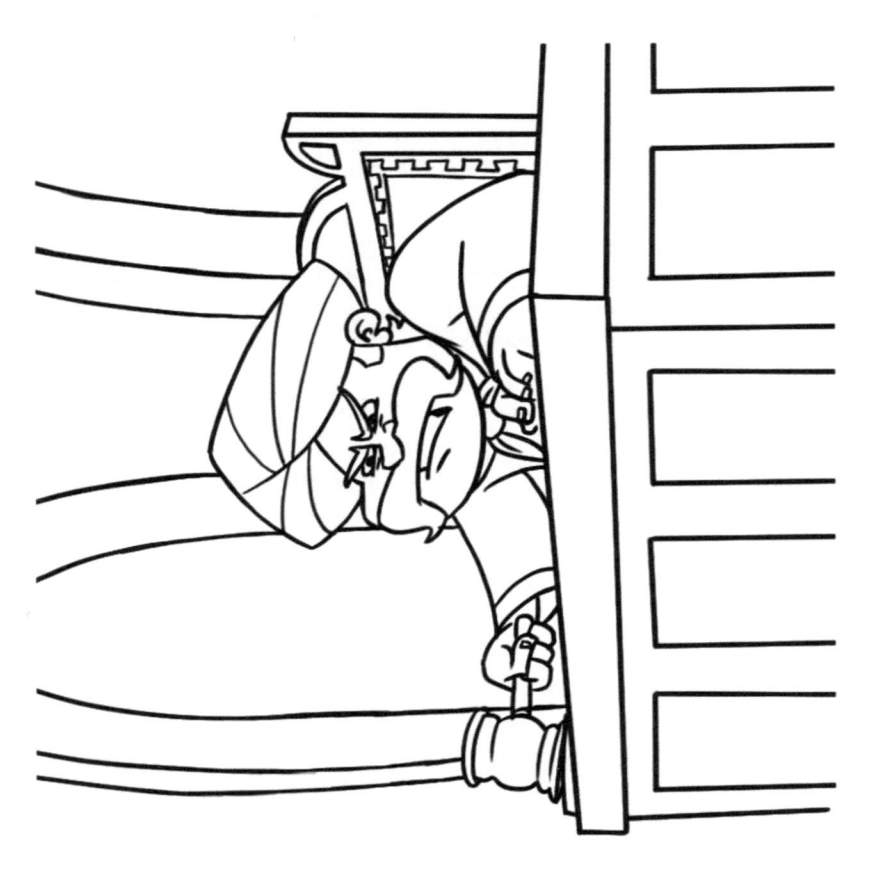

1. When did I last see the object?

2. _____

3. _____

4. _____

5. _____

TAKE-HOME ACTIVITY

NAME: _____

ACTIVITY TWO: TWO SIDES OF BROMAR

Directions to teacher: Make enough copies of the page so that you have enough for each child to have half a page. Cut each page in half and give each child half a page for the previewing activity.

Write five adjectives to describe this person's character

1. _____
2. _____
3. _____
4. _____
5. _____

Write five adjectives to describe this person's character

1. _____
2. _____
3. _____
4. _____
5. _____

IN-CLASS PRE-VIEWING ACTIVITY

NAME: _____

THE SCHOOLMASTER

Story Summary

Shahzaman gets frustrated when he can't figure out his homework. Shahrzad tells him it's not as hard as he thinks. He tells her that's easy for her to say - she's smarter because she's the teacher. Shahrzad tells him that not all teachers know more than their students. In fact, she knows of a teacher who couldn't even read or write. She tells him this story:

Karim and Illya are a pair of con men. They conspire to have Illya take a job as a schoolmaster, even though he is unable to read or write. They figure he can fool everyone for a month and then abscond with his paycheck before anyone figures out he's a fraud. Illya manages to pull it off by having the smarter kids teach the others. The kids love it, and soon, word spreads among the parents that Illya is the best schoolmaster the town has ever had. Things catch up with him, however, when he and Karim are finally revealed as con men by one of the people they cheated. Instead of running, however, Illya steps forward and gives back the money. He learns the value of honesty from his own students, and in the end, he even learns to read.

Story Lessons
- Help children understand that lying is wrong and that it is never too late to become an honest person.
- Encourage children to see the benefits of a good education.
- Encourage children to recognize their own potential to teach and to share their skills and knowledge, and to see themselves as resources for one another.

CLASS PLAN

Pre-Viewing Activity (Approximately 5 Minutes)

Imagine there is something you really want. You can get it if you tell a lie, and you won't get caught! Would you tell the lie? Why or why not? Have a discussion about the consequences of lying. Telling the truth is more about doing the right thing, respecting others (and yourself), and creating a community based on honesty than it is about not getting caught.

Then, if you have not done so already, have a discussion about how people who tell lies eventually do, in fact, get caught.

Watch or Read Episode (Approximately 10 Minutes)

Post-Viewing Discussion Questions (Approximately 10 Minutes)

Why does Illya accept the job of the schoolmaster, even though he cannot read? Why does he finally admit the truth?
(*Discussion:* At first, Illya thinks that lying and stealing are okay, so he accepts the job of schoolmaster, even though he's not qualified and can't read. He is convinced that fooling the students and town is not a problem. But as he sees that his students and the town look up to him, even though he doesn't deserve it, he comes to realize that his actions are wrong and have been harming the students, whom he genuinely appreciates.)

Why is it wrong to be dishonest with others?
(*Discussion:* By lying to others, you are not treating them or yourself with respect, and you are not behaving toward them the way you'd like them to behave toward you. Dishonesty often becomes a bad habit, so the person lying feels it is okay to tell more lies. Not only do these lies make the person feel bad about him or herself, they also make others less trustful in general. Lying erodes trust between you and others, and this distrust has the cumulative effect of eroding trust within the larger community.)

Why is it important to learn to read?
(*Discussion:* Reading is a valuable life skill that makes it possible to learn new information about the world, to communicate with others, and to read stories that teach and entertain. At the end of the episode, Illya tries to better himself by learning to read.)

What do you think would have happened if Illya ran off and did not give the money back at the end?
(*Discussion:* If Illya had run off with the money, he probably would have been caught, and probably would have faced harsh consequences, such as jail. He then would not have learned to read or earned the respect of the townspeople. The consequences for the town would have been negative as well. They would have no teacher for the students, and would stop trusting people. Finally, the students would have been hurt, because someone they looked up to would have cheated them.)

In-Class Activity – for 50-60 Minute Lessons (Approximately 30 Minutes)

In this story, a character pretends to have experience and expertise that he doesn't, in fact, have. Have students work in pairs or small groups to create short plays (about five to ten minutes long), which adhere to the following structure:

Scene 1: A character goes to a job interview for an important job for which he or she is NOT qualified and has NO experience, such as being the architect for a new bridge, a doctor in a children's hospital, or a cook in a restaurant. The person who is hiring offers lots of money and perks. The person interviewing for the job lies and says they are qualified and have experience. They are hired.

Scene 2: When "on the job" and things go horribly wrong, how do they react?

Scene 3: The character either (a) is caught, fired, and arrested OR (b) admits the truth and offers to help fix the mess they caused.

Use the activities to generate discussions on the consequences of lying in each situation and generally in society.

At the start of the story, Illya and his friend, Karim, think that it is all right to trick the waitress, so they can get food without paying for it. They also think that it is fine for Illya to take a job as a schoolteacher, even though he cannot read. They do these things because they have certain beliefs about lying. Fill in the blanks to show what was going through Illya's mind when he made those decisions.

I used to think that it's okay to lie because I thought:

- My needs were more important than other people's.

• _____
• _____
• _____

At the end of the story, Illya learns that honest, hard work is the only way to learn and to grow as a person.

I now know that being honest is the right way because:

- Lies DO hurt other people.

• _____
• _____
• _____

TAKE-HOME ACTIVITY

NAME: _____

ACTIVITY TWO: SCHOOLTEACHER FOR A DAY

One of the more powerful moments from this episode is when Illya's students feel empowered by teaching others. Everyone has talents and knowledge that they can share with others.

Directions: Pick a topic or hobby that you are interested in. Fill in the chart below to create a lesson plan. Teach a short lesson to your family about the topic you selected. Maybe you can teach others about the history of your favorite sport, or give a lesson about how one of your heroes overcame obstacles to succeed. Other examples include teaching others how to draw familiar objects or sharing the results of an at-home science experiment, the facts about deep-sea ocean creatures or a foreign language you are learning.

Topic: _____

Three questions about your topic that your lesson will answer:

1. _____

2. _____

3. _____

Describe a fun activity your students can do to learn the information:

_____

_____

_____

How did it turn out? How successful were you as a teacher?

_____

_____

TAKE-HOME ACTIVITY

NAME: _____

MASTERPIECE

Story Summary

An artist named Manee is trying to sell his paintings in the town square when another artist, Navid, sets up next to him. Manee tells him to go someplace else because this spot is his. Navid accommodates him and moves to the other side of the square. He immediately starts selling paintings. Annoyed, Manee goes to him and tells him he wants to trade spots. Navid once again lets Manee have his way and switches places with him. To Manee's surprise, Navid once again sells his paintings, while Manee has no customers. Angry, Manee orders Navid to leave the square altogether. Navid refuses, and the men get into a fight, spraying each other with paint. In the process, their paintings get covered with bright splotches of paint. To their surprise, people love this new kind of art, and they begin to buy up all their paintings. Realizing they have something that sells, the two men join forces and become wealthy together as partners.

Story Lessons

- Encourage children to understand that when two people are opposed, they have a lot to gain by working together. Through cooperation, they can often achieve a win-win solution. Unity creates strength.
- Help children understand that they usually have more things in common with their competitors than they realize.

CLASS PLAN

Pre-Viewing Activity (Approximately 5 Minutes)

Tell the class you will be playing a numbers game that will require five volunteers. The goal is to have the five people call out all the numbers from one to five. However, they must follow the following rules: (1) Each person must only say one number, (2) the numbers may not be called in numerical order, and (3) the numbers may not be called at the same time. Ask for the five volunteers. Tell them they will play this game twice. The first time, the five people have to close their eyes, and sit in a big circle with their backs to one another. They are not allowed to talk to one another before they start counting. They will discover that without planning or visual cues, students will probably overlap on numbers or at least be hesitant to speak up. Now repeat the game, but this time give them two minutes to talk and plan before they begin. Which way was easier? Have a discussion about the benefits of working together.

As you watch/read this story, look for ways that the two main characters learn to stop being opponents and become cooperative friends and successful business partners.

Watch or Read Episode (Approximately 3 Minutes)

Note: this episode is only 3 minutes long and contains no dialogue.

Post-Viewing Discussion Questions (Approximately 10 Minutes)

Why were Manee and Navid fighting?
(*Discussion:* Both men are street artists, trying to make their living selling paintings to people who pass by. Each man believes that if the other sells a painting, they are losing a sale, and therefore, the other is preventing him from being successful.)

Why did Manee and Navid stop fighting? What did they realize?
(*Discussion:* These men discovered, in the end, that by working together, they were able to achieve greater success than either did separately. Plus, they had a more enjoyable time in the process.)

Some people say that cooperation is an important key to success. Do you agree? Why or why not? Can you think of a time in your own life when cooperation helped you?
(*Discussion:* People often want different things. Sometimes it is difficult to find a solution that will satisfy everyone. Sometimes the key to resolving conflicts or disagreements is searching for compromises.)

In-Class Activity – for 50-60 Minute Lessons (Approximately 30 Minutes)

To help students understand that there is strength in unity and cooperation, have them do the following activity:

Create a Creature

Divide students into groups of three. Give each group a piece of blank paper that is folded into thirds lengthwise. Explain that the three students will be creating an unusual creature that has three different-looking parts. Each student will be creating only one part. Say that each child will keep their third of the creature's body hidden until the end. The first student's job is to secretly draw the HEAD of the creature on the top portion of the page and then overlap the lines of the neck to the second section. Without seeing the section of the paper that the first student drew, the second student is instructed to draw the creature's BODY on the second panel. The panel is then folded, and the paper is given to the third student. Without being able to see the drawings of the first or second student, the third student is given the folded paper and told to draw the LEGS. The teacher then takes the paper and unfolds it to show the final picture.

Now, redo the exercise, but this time, permit the second student to see the portion drawn by the first student, and the third to see the work of the first and second students before drawing their sections. Was there a difference in the final outcome? Engage in a discussion about the benefits of cooperating and working together.

ACTIVITY ONE: HOW WE ARE ALIKE

It is sometimes easy to focus on how people are different from each other than how we are alike. In this activity, challenge yourself to find ways that you and someone you think of as very different from you, might share some things in common.

In the half circle on the left ("ME") write five things that you like to do for fun. In the circle on the right ("YOU"), write the name of the other person and then five different things that this person does for fun, activities that you do not enjoy. Then in the middle, write down three things that you both have in common. When you try, you will often find that you have more in common with others than you think!

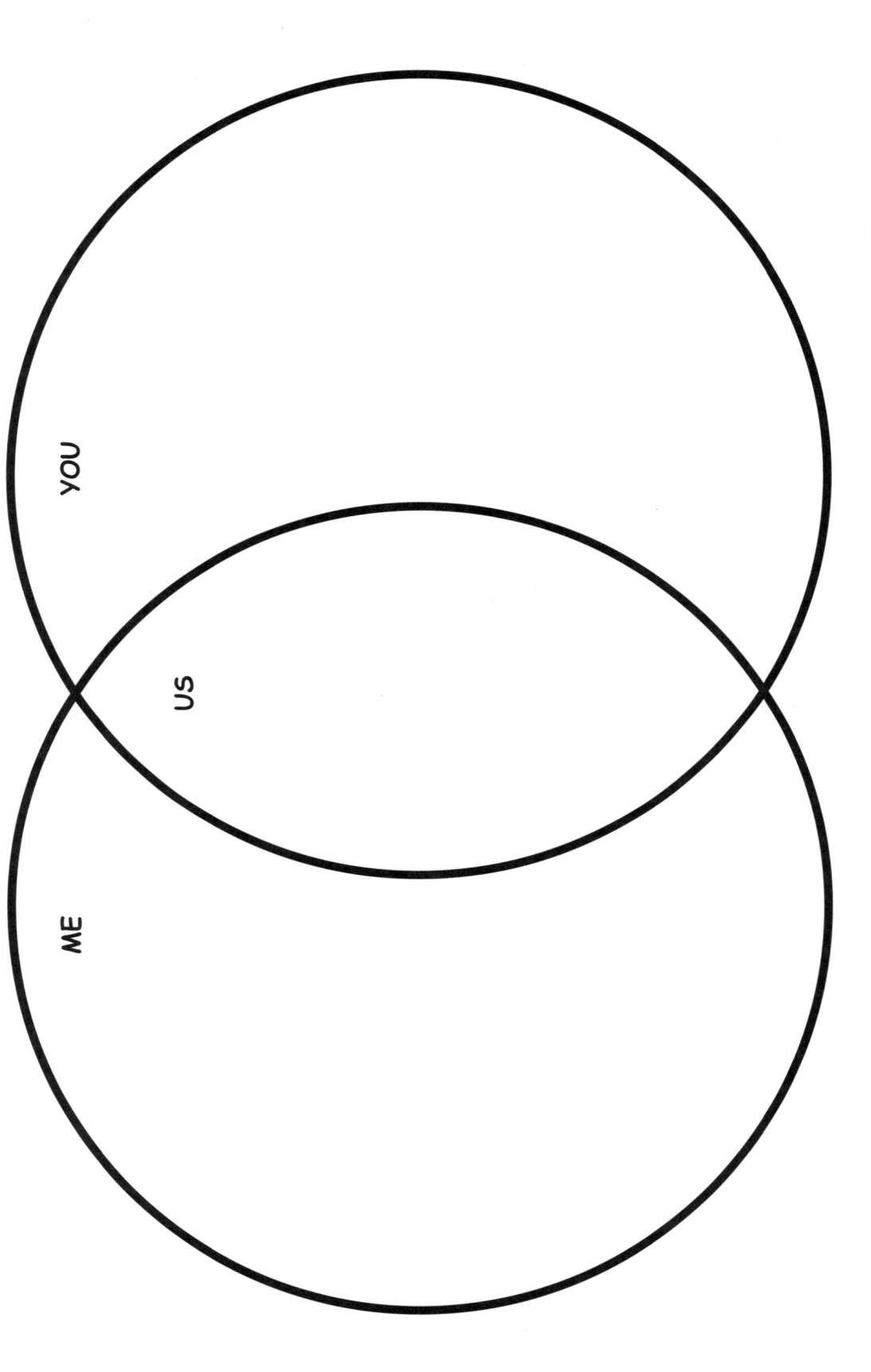

ME

US

YOU

TAKE-HOME ACTIVITY

NAME: _____

WHICH WAY IS UP?

Note: Prior to class, teachers will need to make multiple copies of The Pre-Viewing Activity Sheet, which is attached to the back of this Lesson Plan.

Story Summary

When Shahryar and his cousin Darius argue over the proper way to eat an ear of corn, Shahrzad points out the silliness of their quarrel. She tells them a story of two brothers who once got into a terrible argument that divided their entire family:

When their land is hit by drought, two brothers, Joshua and Daniel, are told by their ailing father to seek out a better place on top of the great mountain, where there are lakes filled with fish and trees brimming with fruit. They lead their family across the desert to the base of the great mountain, but when they arrive, they find there are two paths leading up. Interpreting their father's message differently, Joshua and Daniel argue over which is the right path to take. The family descends into a quarrel, and they split into two groups. Each group takes a different path, certain the others will meet with destruction. They all endure hardships along the way, but in the end, they arrive at the same place. The two sides reconcile their differences and embrace each other. They realize that there is not just one correct path in life. They also learn that one person's beliefs can be different from another's, yet both can be valid and correct.

Story Lessons

- Encourage children to realize that there is often more than one "right" way to achieve a goal. Flexible thinking is often the key to success.
- Encourage children to be tolerant of the beliefs and ideas of others, even though they may be different from their own perspectives or belief systems.
- Help children realize that arguing is not an effective way to resolve a disagreement.
- Provide children with positive strategies for resolving a quarrel with a sibling a friend.

CLASS PLAN

Pre-Viewing Activity (Approximately 5 Minutes)

Present each student with a handout of a simple maze (attached to the end of this lesson plan as Pre-Viewing Activity). One end of the maze reads "start," and the other reads "finish." As noted below, there are two routes to the end of the maze, one of which requires you to turn right and the other, left. Ask them to take a few minutes to see if they can solve it.

Ask students to share how they got from one end to the other. How many people feel that they should first turn left? How many feel the correct path requires them to first turn right? They'll soon discover that the maze has more than one right answer. Explain that sometimes in life, problems have more than one solution. Encourage them to think of examples. There might, for example, be many right answers to "What should we eat for lunch?" or "Where might be an interesting country to visit?" or "What gift should we give a friend for his or her birthday?"

Watch or Read Episode (Approximately 10 Minutes)

Post-Viewing Discussion Questions (Approximately 10 Minutes)

Why do you think the two brothers, in either the frame story or the flashback story, are arguing?
(*Discussion:* The brothers are quarrelling because each one thinks he is right. They don't realize that, in life, there is often more than one way to do something, and more than one person can be right.)

What advice would you tell them to help the brothers stop fighting?
(*Discussion:* Each of the brothers should try to be more open-minded and listen to each other's ideas. They want their opinions to be respected, so they should offer the same courtesy to each other.)

What did the brothers think their father's dream meant?
(*Discussion:* Each brother interpreted his father's dream from only his own perspective. They did not listen to each other's point of view. Each brother followed his own perspective of what their father said, and eventually, they found the promised land, but at the cost of upsetting and disrupting their family.)

What was the cost of each brother not listening and fighting with the other?
(*Discussion:* It placed tension on the family, and their quest split the family.)

Do you disagree sometimes with your family members/friends? What topics cause differences of opinion? How do you resolve these conflicts?
(*Discussion:* Answers will vary based on students' experiences.)

In-Class Activity – for 50-60 Minute Lessons (Approximately 30 Minutes)

Divide the class into two teams. Each team works independently for about eight to ten minutes to come up with ten different questions, each of which has more than one right answer. Examples include:

- What is the most delicious meal you can imagine?
- What is the best sport in the world?
- What is the most boring thing to do in the world?
- What is the best way to do well in school?
- If you could only listen to one song for the rest of your life, what would it be?

Then each team reads one of its questions to the other team—and the other team has a limited amount of time (about two minutes) to come up with as many answers to the question as possible. The team answering the question gets one point for each answer suggested. Then the teams switch roles – with the 'question asking team' now providing as many answers as possible.

The teacher should ask if there are any right answers and wrong answers to these questions and then explain that while some questions and answers have right and wrong answers, when it comes to beliefs, there are only opinions –and nothing is right or wrong. Teachers should then explain the importance of respecting other people's beliefs.

ACTIVITY ONE: RESPECTING DIFFERENT BELIEFS

In this episode, Joshua and Daniel fight about which is the right path to take to get to the top of the mountain. At the end, they discover there is often more than one right answer to a problem.

Directions: Tell a family member or friend about how the two brothers in this episode divided their family due to a disagreement about what they believed they heard.

Disagreements about facts can almost always be resolved, but differences in beliefs cannot. Below are four examples of disagreements. Read the first two examples, and then in the third and fourth, write the type of disagreement and how it may be resolved. In the fifth spot, come up with an example of a disagreement, tell whether it is a disagreement of fact or belief, and write a possible solution.

1. Situation: Two people disagree about who is taller.
   Type of Disagreement: Factual
   Solution: Have a third person use a measuring tape to measure who is taller.

2. Situation: Two people disagree about which dessert tastes better.
   Type of Disagreement: Belief
   Solution: Understand that people can believe different things, and we should respect one another's beliefs.

3. Situation: Two people disagree about what kind of animal makes the best pet.
   Type of Disagreement: _____
   Solution: _____

4. Situation: Two people disagree about the distance from home to school.
   Type of Disagreement: _____
   Solution: _____

5. Situation: Two people disagree about _____
   Type of Disagreement: _____
   Solution: _____

TAKE-HOME ACTIVITY

NAME: _____

LESSON EIGHTEEN

IS THERE A ROUTE TO THE FINISH WITHOUT CROSSING A LINE?

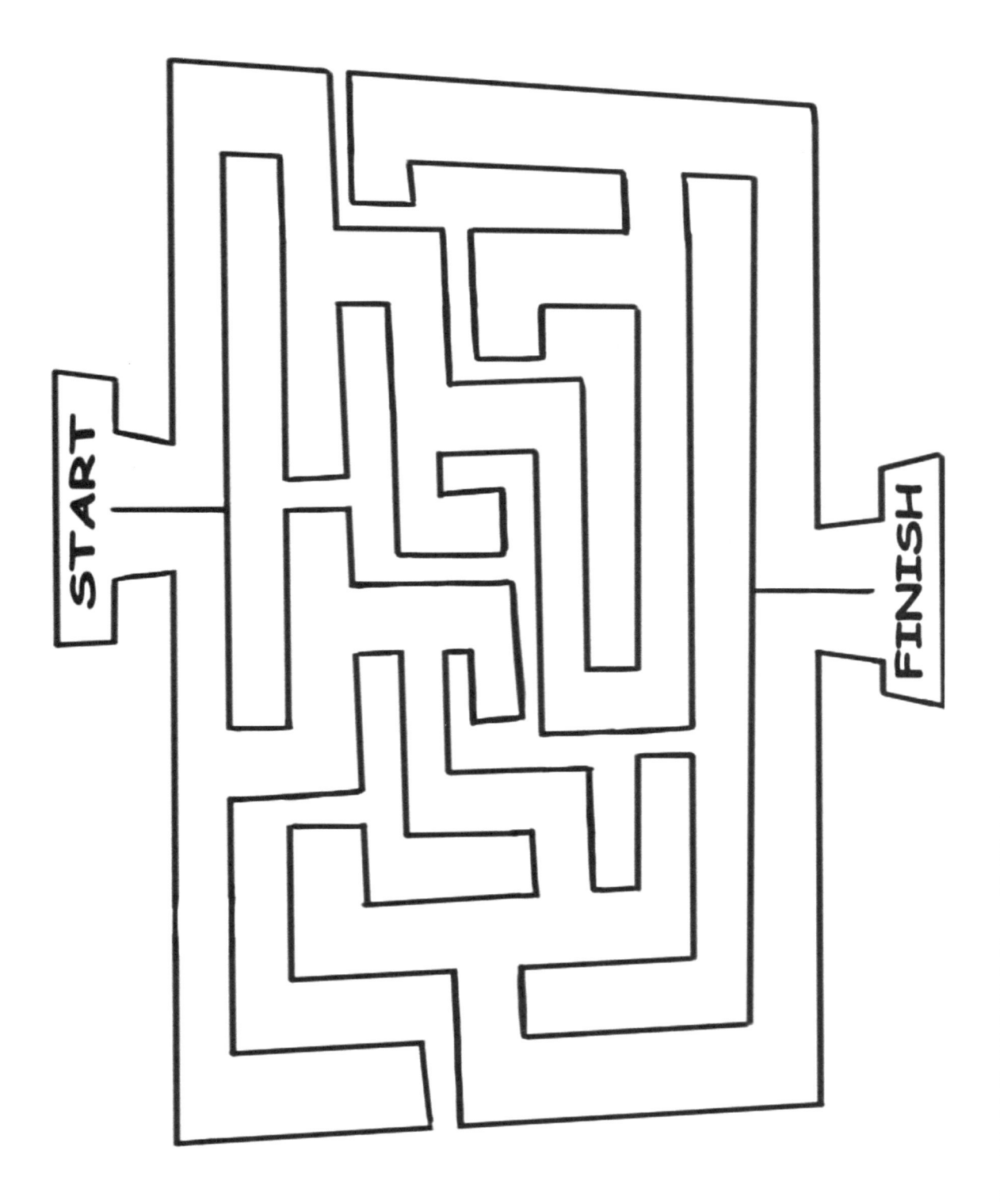

IN-CLASS PRE-VIEWING ACTIVITY

THE GIFT OF NOROOZ

Story Summary

Shahzaman is angry when he doesn't get the gifts he wants for his birthday. Shahrzad points out that the spirit behind the gift is what's important. She tells him this story:

A poor family doesn't have enough money to buy gifts for one another for the Persian holiday of Norooz. They decide instead to each buy one gift for another member of the family. Dad will buy a gift for Mom, Mom will buy a gift for Daughter, Daughter will buy a gift for Brother, Brother will buy a gift for Grandpa, and Grandpa will buy a gift for Dad. Since they have no money, they each sell something in order to buy a gift. On the day of Norooz, Mom receives a fresh bale of cotton from Dad to use on her spinning wheel, but it turns out she sold her spinning wheel in order to buy her daughter a present. Her daughter receives new paints, but she sold her paintbrushes in order to buy her brother a tool belt. Her brother loves the tool belt for storing his tools, but he sold his tools in order to buy Grandpa a new pair of reading glasses. Grandpa is delighted to be able to read his books now, but he sold his books in order to buy Dad a new backgammon table. Dad loves the table, but he sold his backgammon board in order to buy Mom the cotton! It turns out they each got a present they cannot use! A stranger appears at the door, and it turns out to be old Amoo Norooz himself. The family soon learns the true spirit of giving in the best Norooz celebration ever.

Story Lessons
- Encourage children to appreciate any gifts from others and to realize that it's the thought that counts.
- Inspire children to make and appreciate homemade gifts, rather than expensive store-bought gifts, to celebrate special occasions.
- Encourage children to realize that the love of family and friends is the most precious gift of all.
- Encourage children to appreciate the importance of putting the needs and wants of others before your own.

CLASS PLAN

Pre-Viewing Activity (Approximately 5 Minutes)

Ask the students: Do the best gifts always cost a lot of money? Have students brainstorm a list of inexpensive gifts they could make for a friend or family member's birthday. They should cost little or no money. Encourage them to think of a drawing or painting they could make, a special meal they could prepare, a homemade "gift certificate" good for hugs, and so on. Ask students to discuss how they would feel if they received these types of gifts.

Watch or Read Episode (Approximately 10 Minutes)

Post-Viewing Discussion Questions (Approximately 10 Minutes)

When the family members all realize that they can't use the gifts they received, they laugh and say, "Are we ridiculous or what?" Why do you think they laughed? If this situation had happened to you, how do you think you might have reacted?
(*Discussion:* One reason they laughed is that they appreciated the fact that the others had made sacrifices for their happiness. Most students will find it nice that each sacrificed something important to them in order to do something that pleases someone they love.)

Why did the daughter sell her paintbrushes, even though she loved painting? Similarly, why did the grandfather, who loves to read, sell his books?
(*Discussion:* The daughter and the grandfather did not mind selling something special they owned, if it meant they could make a loved one happier.)

Talk about a time in your life when you gave something special away to someone you cared about.
(*Discussion:* This may vary depending on students' experiences. Emphasize the benefits of selfless behavior and point out that kind behavior toward others is often rewarded in unexpected ways.)

In-Class Activity – for 50-60 Minute Lessons (Approximately 30 Minutes)

To celebrate the spirit of simple gift giving, and helping others, the class can create simple artworks in class. They could make a simple pencil holder by covering and decorating a tin can, or by using the bottom half of a plastic bottle to make a flowerpot. Other suggestions for homemade artwork:

- Drawing a welcome sign for the front door
- Painting a picture with the words "I love you"
- A clay sculpture of two people hugging
- Simple origami of animals
- Drawing of a tree that is growing red hearts
- A homemade castle made from an old cardboard box

When they are completed, students give them to someone in their lives. It doesn't have to be for a special occasion, such as a birthday, but could simply be to tell the other person they love them.

ACTIVITY ONE: EACH VASE IS SPECIAL

LESSON NINETEEN

Directions: In this episode, the family members work together to create a beautiful homemade vase as a gift. Now it's your turn. With a family member at home, color and cut out a paper vase, using the handout given. When you are done, tape the vase into a shape that stands up and color it.

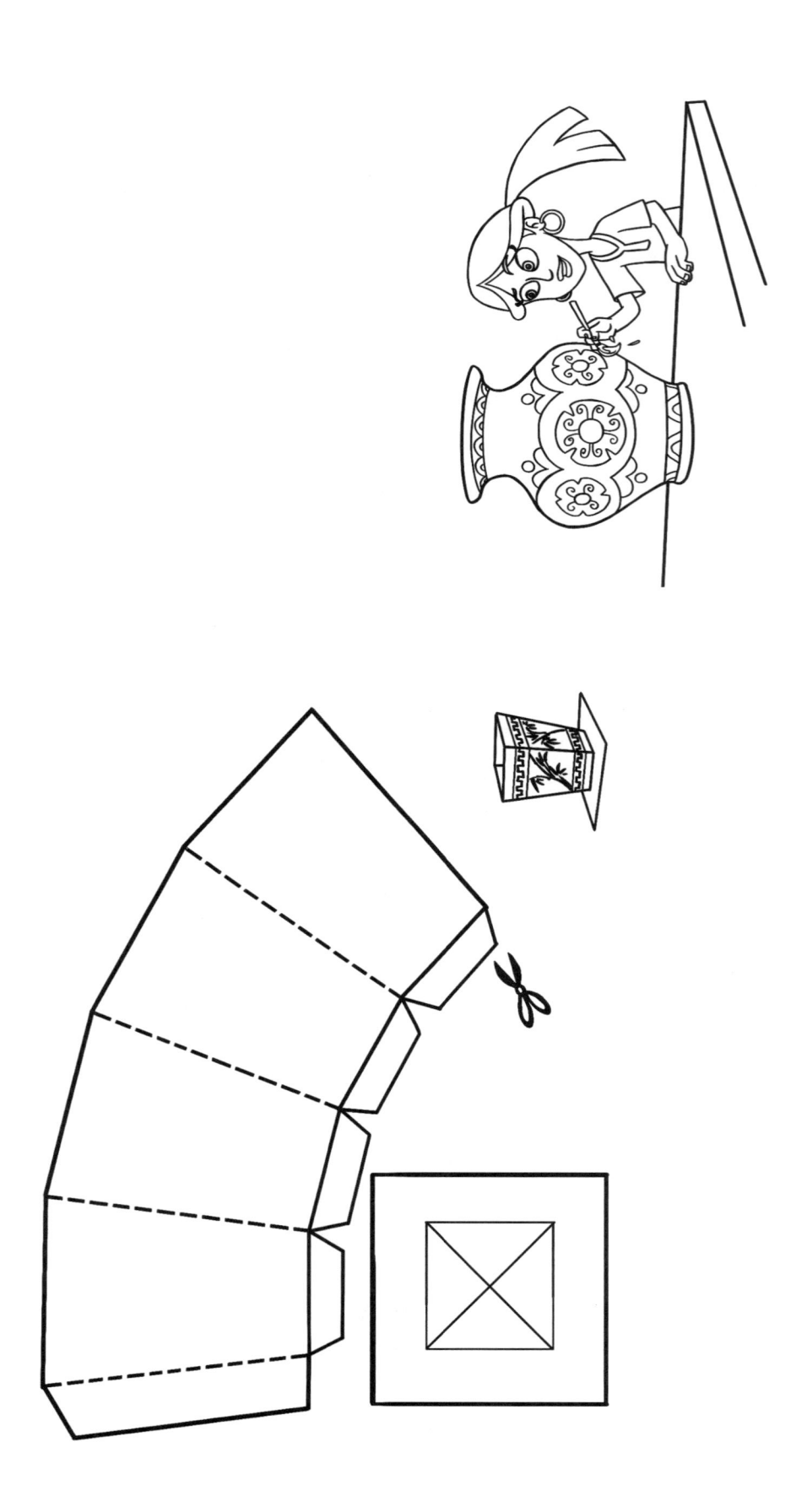

TAKE-HOME ACTIVITY

NAME: _____

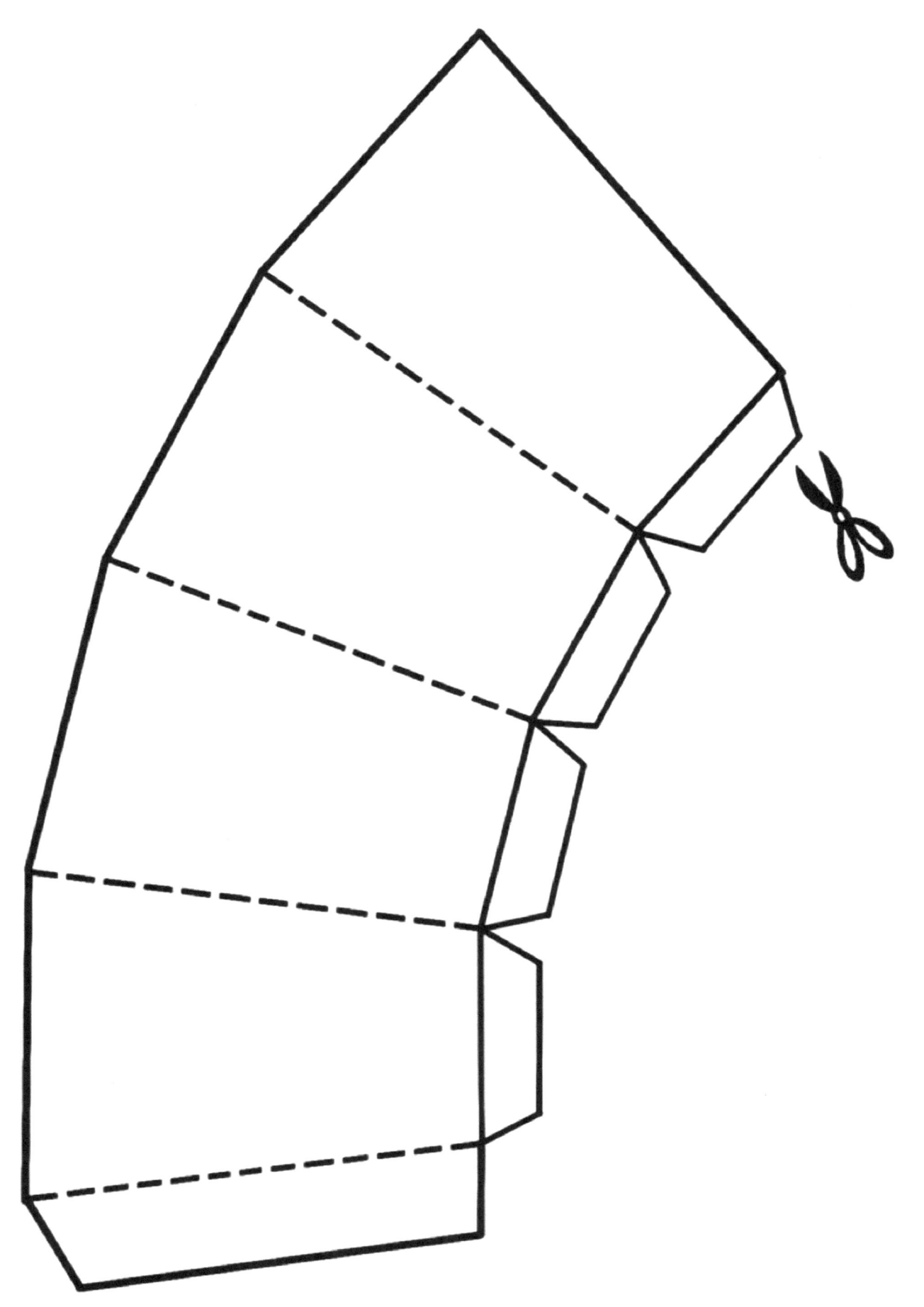

JUST MY LUCK

Story Summary

A statue of Shahryar is accidentally knocked over and breaks into pieces. Shahryar bemoans his bad luck, but Shahrzad explains that bad luck can sometimes be good luck. She tells him this story:

A man named Shandar suffered from bad luck all his life. As a child, his brother left home and never came back. Now as an adult, Shandar's business has failed, and he's moving to a new town to get a fresh start. On the way, his wagon breaks down. He regards this as more bad luck as he's forced to take a detour to the nearest town to get the wheel fixed. On the way, he finds a locked box on the road and takes it with him. When he gets to town, the blacksmith is busy repairing another wagon, so Shandar has to wait. He manages to open the locked box and finds money inside. At last, good luck! Only it turns into bad luck, because the money was stolen, and Shandar is now accused of being the thief. He's locked in jail. He escapes, but as bad luck would have it, he's caught and brought before the judge. During the trial, the blacksmith appears and explains that the wagon he was fixing had a loose board. This means the box of money fell out of the wagon and Shandar wasn't lying; he actually found it and did not steal it. Shandar is set free. When he hears the blacksmith's name, it turns out to be his long-lost brother. Shandar realizes that because his wagon broke down, it forced him to come to this strange town. When he was arrested, it brought the blacksmith forward. Everything Shandar thought was bad luck was really a path to good luck, because it reunited him with his long-lost brother.

Story Lessons
- Help children realize that innocent people are sometimes unfairly accused of things they did not do. When this happens, it is important to state the truth and to persist until justice is achieved.
- Help children understand that people should be presumed to be innocent until the facts prove guilt.
- Explain that everyone has good and bad luck, but that good and bad luck is about perspective. Additionally, lucky people are often those that let the bad things go and work hard for good things to happen. If bad things happen to you, don't dwell on them; be strong and try harder —good things can be achieved.

CLASS PLAN

Pre-Viewing Activity (Approximately 5 Minutes)

To help children explore the notion that one's perspective can affect how one looks at things, ask for four student volunteers and have them stand in this arrangement in front of the class:

Observer 1

Student A   Student B

Observer 2

Ask Observer 1: Who is standing on the left? Student A or Student B (using the students' real names)? Then ask the same question to Observer 2. Ask the class: Which student's answer is correct? Point out that both answers are correct for each student.

Ask students if they have ever had something bad lead them to something that was good? You might share an example from personal experience. For example, perhaps you took a wrong turn while driving to a friend's house, and got lost. But when you ended up in a new neighborhood, you met a new friend, who helped you get back on track. Tell them that they are about to hear or watch a story about perspective.

Watch or Read Episode (Approximately 10 Minutes)

Post-Viewing Discussion Questions (Approximately 10 Minutes)

If someone is accused of a crime he or she did not commit, what should that person do?
(*Discussion:* Like Shandar in this episode, it is important to keep speaking the truth and seek out any evidence, eye-witnesses, and logical arguments that help prove one's innocence.)

Some people believe "The harder I work, the luckier I get." Do you agree or disagree with this idea? Give your reasons.
(*Discussion:* Many people believe that if they keep trying and working toward their goals, they will have more good things happen to them than bad. For example, a student who studies hard before a test will have more "luck" during the test than a student who didn't study much. The truth is that luck has little to do with it; this student is just better prepared.)

Why are rumors dangerous in a community? If you heard a rumor that made a bad assumption about someone else, what should you do?
(*Discussion:* Rumors are dangerous because they aren't based on truth—but people spread the bad news, anyway. If you heard some bad news about someone else, do not mention it to others unless you have proof of what happened.)

In-Class Activity – for 50-60 Minute Lessons (Approximately 30 Minutes)

Discuss how good and bad things happen every day. Spend five minutes brainstorming some examples of each and writing them down on the board. When you ask someone if they had a lucky day or not, the person's response often has to do with their perspective – which events does the person focus more on: those that lead to positive events or those that lead to negative outcomes. Often, it is easy to focus only on things that go wrong and think of oneself as "unlucky."

Have students try to remember some of the "lucky" and "unlucky" things that happened to them during the past week. Write down the responses on the board. It is important to emphasize that the good things need not be big (e.g., finding a pot of gold or discovering a long-lost brother). Sometimes little things, like good weather or the chance to play a game with a good friend, can feel lucky.

Discuss the idea that if you believe in yourself, and work hard toward achieving your goals, good things will seem to "happen" to you. (The opposite perspective is, of course, also true.) What we call good luck is actually good preparation and persistence.

ACTIVITY ONE: I AM INNOCENT!

Have you ever been accused of doing something wrong that you didn't do? Talk with a family member about your experience, and together write down the details of what happened. Turn this story into a short comic strip — with make-believe characters.

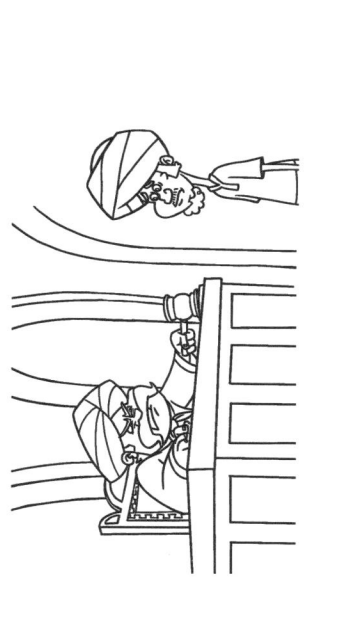

Some suggestions for your comic:

* Make it clear why one person thinks the other person is guilty.
* Have the accused person stick to the strategy of saying over and over again, "But I am telling the truth!" Do you think this would convince other people? What might work better?
* At the end of the comic, have the person who accused the other person of the crime apologize for their mistake.

TAKE-HOME ACTIVITY

NAME: _____

ACTIVITY TWO: HARD WORK LEADS TO "GOOD LUCK"

In this episode, Shandar thinks of himself as an "unlucky" person. His cart breaks down, he is accused of a crime he didn't do, and more. The truth is that he didn't put in the effort to take care of his cart so that it wouldn't break down. He could have also had the tools to repair his cart and to continue on his journey. His discovery of his long-lost brother is actually a happy coincidence rather than good luck.

Many people believe that hard work on a goal leads to more good luck. Try this idea for yourself. If you can, have a family member help you fill out this form.

1. PICK A GOAL FOR THIS WEEK. It might be doing well on a test at school, or making a new friend, or trying to eat healthier food. WRITE THE GOAL HERE:

   _____

2. HOW LUCKY DO YOU THINK YOU'LL BE? Decide how lucky you think you'll be when trying to achieve this goal. Pick a number between one through five (five being "very lucky" and one being "very unlucky)."

3. WRITE DOWN THREE EXAMPLES OF WAYS YOU COULD WORK HARD TOWARD ACHIEVING THIS GOAL. TRY TO ACHIEVE THE GOAL.

4. DID YOU ACHIEVE THE GOAL NAD WERE YOU LUCKY? At the end of the week, pick another number (between one through five) that shows how lucky you felt that past week.

5. THINK ABOUT WHY YOU DID OR DID NOT SUCCEED. If you succeeded, were you lucky or did you work hard? If you did not succeed, were you unlucky, or could you have worked harder or done something differently?

TAKE-HOME ACTIVITY

NAME: _____

THE TALE OF TAYMOUR AND TINY

Story Summary

Donyazad is afraid of a spider, and Shahrzad explains how spiders can help us. For example, they catch bothersome flies for food. Shahrzad goes on to explain that several animals have symbiotic relationships with humans. She tells Donyazad this story:

In ancient Persia, there was a small town plagued by snakes. A boy named Taymour was practicing driving them away with his slingshot when his mother told him to stop, because it was dangerous. When she wasn't looking, however, Taymour tried to hit a pinecone high in a tree, and instead, he knocked an egg out of a bird's nest. Unable to put back the egg, Taymour hatched it inside the henhouse and named his new bird Tiny. Tiny soon grew to be more than ten feet tall and had a ravenous appetite. Fearing Tiny would become a menace, the townspeople ordered Taymour to get rid of the bird. As they tried to drive Tiny away, however, snakes attacked the cornfields and began gobbling up their crops. Tiny went after the snakes and ate them like a normal bird eats worms. Overjoyed, the townspeople now welcomed Tiny to stay. They were surprised when a huge rukh bird appeared, and it turned out to be Tiny's mother. Thinking they had stolen her baby, the rukh almost devoured the townspeople when Tiny stopped her. Seeing that these people were kind to her baby, the mother left them alone and flew off with Tiny to join the rest of the rukh birds. From that day forward, the rukh birds protected the townspeople from snakes, and the humans and rukh birds lived together in harmony.

Story Lessons

- Encourage children to take responsibility for their actions.
- Encourage children to be kind to animals, to see how different animals are interconnected and serve many useful purposes for people.
- Inspire children to feel empathy for those who are less fortunate.
- Encourage children to see the good in others, rather than focusing on the negative.

CLASS PLAN

Pre-Viewing Activity (Approximately 5 Minutes)

Ask students to imagine they are walking down the street, and they find a coin. They pick it up, put it in their pocket, and feel lucky! A minute later, they find another coin, then another, then another, and then another. That's strange to discover so much money on the sidewalk. A few minutes later, they see someone walking down the street carrying a bag that is accidentally leaking money. What do they do?

Discuss various actions one might take. What would it feel like to be the person who was losing all those coins, but didn't realize it? How would it feel to be the person to return the dropped coins to their owner?

Talk about what it means to take responsibility for your actions. Point out that doing this is sometimes hard, but it is the right thing to do.

Watch or Read Episode (Approximately 10 Minutes)

Post-Viewing Discussion Questions (Approximately 10 Minutes)

How would you define "responsibility"?
(*Discussion:* Responsibility involves being dependable and accountable. If you make a mistake, you honestly admit it and take action to right any wrongs. A good example might be doing your chores without being told or cleaning up after yourself.)

When the egg falls out of the tree, how does Taymour take responsibility for his actions?
(*Discussion:* Since Taymour caused the egg to fall out of its nest, he realized that it was his responsibility to take care of it. Knowing he couldn't put the egg back in the tall tree, Taymour decided to put the egg in a nest with his family's chickens. When the bird hatched, he took responsibility for feeding it and caring for it. Make sure all students understand what "responsibility" means.)

Shahrzad says we should all help one another in some way, so we can live in harmony. Can you think of some ways that people in our community can help one another?
(*Discussion:* Answers will vary based on students' responses, but make sure to discuss how members of the community with more money and other resources have a responsibility to help those less fortunate. Children can help their teachers and school by respecting one another's property and feelings. Point out that communities have many different groups of people in them. Communities and societies are successful only when the people in them work together to solve problems and accept cultural differences.)

In-Class Activity – for 50-60 Minute Lessons (Approximately 30 Minutes)

To help children focus on positive qualities in one another, have students work in pairs. Each child needs to tell the class three good things about the other. Have the students spend a few minutes to prepare for their presentations. They might point out things such as a student's smile, talk about one of his or her hobbies, or point out something nice that the student did to help a friend or family member.

As a class, select an area near your school that has a lot of litter. Bring bags, gloves, and any other supplies you think you will need. Work together to clean up the area. You might want to take photographs or draw pictures to show what the area looked like before and after.

ACTIVITY ONE: DON'T JUMP TO CONCLUSIONS

What is Taymour up to? Some people who don't know him well will look at this picture of him and think he's doing something wrong. Other people who know him well will look at him and realize he's doing something special for a friend. Work with a family member to fill in the chart below.

What Does It Look Like Taymour Is Doing?	What Is Taymour REALLY Doing?

Can you think of a time when you jumped to conclusions about someone you didn't know well?

_____

_____

How did it feel when you learned the truth?

_____

_____

TAKE-HOME ACTIVITY

NAME: _____

ACTIVITY TWO: THE POWER OF BEING RESPONSIBLE

Do you ever wish you had more power? One of the ways adults will often give you more power is if you show that you are responsible. What does this mean? In the story you saw/read, Taymour took care of the egg when he accidentally knocked it out of the tree. What are some ways that you could be more responsible?

Talk with a family member to think of some examples of what a responsible person might do. Think about times, for example, when you didn't walk away from something difficult or awkward. Then read this list and add your own ideas.

- Don't make excuses for mistakes you made. If you spill something, make sure you are the one to clean it up.

- Make a list of things your parents or other grown-ups ask you to do, such as brushing your teeth or making your bed. Then see if you can do these things BEFORE a grown-up has to remind you.

- Show compassion for others. If you see someone look sad, or even crying, talk to that person to see what's wrong and if there is anything you can do to help.

- Stick by your promises. When you say you are going to do something to help out, make sure you do it. Otherwise, people will not trust you in the future.

- _____

- _____

TAKE-HOME ACTIVITY

NAME: _____

THE BOY AND THE PANTHER

Story Summary

Donyazad and Shahzaman accidentally knock over a vase while jumping on the bed. When Majid asks who broke it, they tell him the vase was like that when they found it. Majid blames the maid, but Shahrzad suspects the truth. She tells the kids this story:

When a boy named Nadeem gets a bad report card, his father forbids him to go to the annual county fair. Disobeying his parents, Nadeem sneaks out and goes to the fair, anyway. While there, he secretly witnesses a crime and sees that the wrong person gets arrested for it. He wants to come forward and tell the truth, but if he does, his parents will know he disobeyed them, and he'll get in trouble. He grapples with his conscience and finally makes the right decision. Even though he knows it would get him into trouble, Nadeem tells the truth. In the end, he prevents the wrong person from going to prison, and he's grounded for three months.

Story Lessons
- Encourage children to tell the truth, even when doing so may result in punishment.
- Remind children of the importance of obeying their parents.
- Help children understand that teasing animals is cruel and wrong.

CLASS PLAN

Pre-Viewing Activity (Approximately 5 Minutes)

Ask students: How many of you try to tell the truth? Most children will raise their hands. Then say: Now imagine that your mother told you not to drink milk on an expensive carpet, but you did anyway, and then spilled the milk. How many of you would tell the truth? Explain that telling the truth often costs you something, but even in these situations it is important to tell the truth.

Tell the class that as they watch or listen to the story of "The Boy and the Panther," to look or listen for examples of characters lying to each other. See if the lies lead to rewards or punishment.

Watch or Read Episode (Approximately 10 Minutes)

Post-Viewing Discussion Questions (Approximately 10 Minutes)

Why do you think Donyazad and Shahzaman lied and said, "It wasn't us" when asked, "What did you do?" Do you think this was right or wrong? Why?
(*Discussion:* The children didn't want to get into trouble so they lied. They didn't realize that if they had admitted the truth, and apologized, the adults might have been more understanding.)

At the end of the story, Nadeem's father was very angry with Nadeem. When his sister pointed out that what he did took courage, his father still punished him for disobeying him (and going to the fair), but he did reduce the punishment because Nadeem acted courageously. Do you think that his father did the right thing? Why or why not?
(*Discussion:* By telling the truth, Nadeem knew he might get into trouble, so that was courageous, and he did the right thing. His dad punished him because he needed to show Nadeem that what he did was wrong. By reducing Nadeem's punishment, he showed that acting courageously and being truthful will be rewarded.)

What actions do you think parents and teachers could take to encourage children to tell the truth all the time? What actions might get in the way of children telling the truth?
(*Discussion:* If children are somehow rewarded for admitting their mistakes, then they will more likely tell the truth. If children are punished for admitting they did something wrong, they are much less likely to do so.)

If you were in Nadeem's place, what would you have done if you disobeyed your father and went to the fair—and then saw a crime there? If you were Nadeem's father, how might you have reacted to Nadeem's disobeying you but then telling the truth?
(*Discussion:* Since this question asks for the students' opinion, answers will vary. Steer the conversation toward discussing the positive benefits of telling the truth and taking responsibility for one's actions.)

In-Class Activity – for 50-60 Minute Lessons (Approximately 30 Minutes)

When Nadeem sees the wrong person getting blamed for letting the panther out of the cage, he asks himself, "What am I going to do?" Present these examples to the class and discuss what the people in them might do.

Example 1: Two boys are playing football outside. They are having a super time. One of the boys accidentally kicks the football, breaking their neighbor's window. What should the boys do? Should they run away? Should they knock on the neighbor's door to apologize and to tell the truth? What might be the consequences of each approach?

Example 2: A girl borrows a book from a friend. While she is reading it, she discovers some money inside. She really would like to keep it so she can buy some toys. What should she do? Should she keep it and buy the toys? Or should she contact the girl and tell of her discovery? What might be the consequences of each approach?

Invite students to make up a scenario for the others and then end it with something like, "What should the children do?" Follow it with "What might be the consequences of each approach?"

ACTIVITY ONE: AGREEING TO TELL

Parents are usually more understanding when their children tell the truth about doing something wrong. They realize everyone makes mistakes. Fill out this agreement with a parent or adult family member. The goal is to encourage the student to tell the truth to the adult – no matter what. In exchange, the adult promises to be more understanding and give a less-harsh punishment.

I promise to try to tell the truth. If I make a mistake but tell the truth, I hope you will be more understanding.

Child's Name: _____
Child's Signature: _____

If you try to tell the truth, then if you do something wrong I will be more understanding. I will make your punishment less strict if you tell the truth.

Parent's Name: _____
Parent's Signature: _____

TAKE-HOME ACTIVITY

NAME: _____

ABU KASSIM'S SMELLY SHOES

NOTE: Children taking the 50-60 minute class should be instructed, prior to this class, to bring an old object from home that is tattered and used, for the In-Class Activity.

Story Summary

When Shahryar wants to get rid of the family dog because he's old and useless, Shahrzad tells him that old things can save your life. She tells him this story:

A wealthy man named Abu Kassim orders his gardener to get rid of his smelly old shoes. The gardener obeys him, but when he passes away, he bequeaths the shoes to Abu Kassim. Kassim throws away the shoes by tossing them over the wall of his property. They accidentally hit an old woman on the other side and injure her. Kassim is ordered by a judge to pay her damages and is given back the shoes. Kassim then throws the shoes into the river, but they get caught in the rudder of a passing boat, causing it to run aground. He is once again ordered to pay damages and is given back the shoes. Furious, Kassim decides to bury the shoes, but he runs afoul of bandits who had buried stolen loot in the same place. He finally decides to burn the shoes in a bonfire. As the shoes burn, a bird swoops down, grabs the shoes, and flies off with them. Kassim throws a rock at the airborne, flaming shoes, and they drop onto the roof of his house, setting it ablaze. Abu Kassim becomes trapped in the inferno, with no way to escape. With hot coals blocking the way, he puts on the smelly shoes and is able to run across the burning coals to safety. Realizing the shoes had saved his life, Abu Kassim becomes a changed man and wears the shoes for the rest of his life. He learns that even though something is old, it can still be useful.

Story Lessons
- Help children appreciate that all people are equal, deserving of rights and respect, whether they are rich or poor, young or old.
- Help children realize that sometimes things have hidden value that we are not able to immediately understand.

CLASS PLAN

Pre-Viewing Activity (Approximately 5 Minutes)

Show the class three objects that they might otherwise throw away. They could be a piece of paper with scribbles or writing on one side, a paper clip or an old cardboard box. Explain to the class that the objects are going to be taken to a garbage bin. Can they think of any new uses for these old objects? How might these old objects be useful again? Perhaps the piece of paper is crumpled into a ball and is now good for playing catch? Are there any uses they can think of for an old box? How about a paper clip – can you use it as a bookmark for a book, perhaps? Define and discuss the words "reuse" and "recycle."

Explain that as they watch/hear the story, they'll learn of a man who was stuck with an old pair of smelly shoes that he desperately wanted to get rid of.

Watch or Read Episode (Approximately 10 Minutes)

Post-Viewing Discussion Questions (Approximately 10 Minutes)

Why does Abu Kassim think that the old shoes he gets from the old gardener are worthless?
(*Discussion:* Kassim judges objects and people based on their appearances, and he doesn't realize that something, which might be tattered and worn, can still be useful.)

Why did the old lady get hurt? Was it because the shoes were unlucky or because Kassim was inconsiderate?
(*Discussion:* The old lady got hurt because Kassim was inconsiderate. This is also why the boat crashed. He caused his own problems by being inconsiderate of others.)

Did you notice that Abu Kassim didn't know his gardener's name and didn't seem to care about him? Why was this? Was this wrong or right?
(*Discussion:* It was wrong. Abu Kassim is richer, so he felt the old gardener was less important. People are equal whether they are rich or poor.)

Why do you think the old gardener gave his old shoes to Abu Kassim when he (the gardener) died?
(*Discussion:* The elderly gardener appreciated his old shoes and found them very valuable and reliable—so he wanted to give them to his employer when he died, to teach him the value of old things. He wanted to teach the rich man a lesson.)

How do you think Abu Kassim's life would have turned out differently if he had been kind and generous at the start of the story?
(*Discussion:* Chances are, Abu Kassim would have found happiness much earlier in the story, even before the gardener died and gave him the shoes.)

In-Class Activity – for 50-60 Minute Lessons (Approximately 30 Minutes)

As a follow-up to the pre-viewing activity, students are encouraged to bring in one object from home that they feel might be too old to be useful. They could also find an object in the school's recycling area. Note: Alert students to only bring in objects that are safe and sanitary. The teacher should place all the objects in the center of the room and have students take turns taking one of the objects out of the pile that seems interesting. In order to be able to keep the object (and take it home), the object's new owner has to tell the class why the object is useful—and the class has to agree with the student's argument.

Think of some of the oldest members of your community. Interview them to find out what stories, and advice about life, they have.

Below are some questions to get you started, but feel free to ask any questions you think will be useful for learning about their past.

1. What was life like when you were my age?   _____
    _____
    _____

2. Where did you live?   _____

3. What did you do for fun?   _____
    _____
    _____

4. What advice do you have for children today?   _____
    _____
    _____

5. Tell me of a time when you did something brave.   _____
    _____
    _____

TAKE-HOME ACTIVITY   NAME: _____

ACTIVITY TWO: WHEN YOU ARE YOUR GRANDPARENTS' AGE

Many children think of themselves as "forever young." They have a hard time imagining what it would be like to be the age of their grandparents.

Sit down with an adult family member and discuss what life might be like when you are older.

1. How old will you be in 60 years? _____

2. What sorts of things do you think you might be interested in then? _____
    _____
    _____
    _____

3. What will your family be like? _____
    _____
    _____
    _____

4. Will you have a job? If so, what will it be? _____

TAKE-HOME ACTIVITY   NAME: _____

BANDITS OF BASRA

Story Summary

Shahzaman brags to his friends that he's won several soccer trophies. When Donyazad points out to him that he's actually never won a single trophy, he laughs and tells her, "They don't know that." Overhearing this, Shahrzad warns Shahzaman that it's never a good idea to pretend to be something you're not. She tells him this story:

Mujab and Samir are two men who are down on their luck. Desperate for work, they lie to the townspeople of a small village about their credentials in order to take jobs as lawmen. What they don't realize is that the town is being terrorized by a ruthless bandit named Diab. When they're forced to face him, they run away like cowards, leaving the town helpless. Ashamed of themselves, they return the next day to take on Diab and his men. Faced with certain death, they are aided at the last minute by real lawmen who show up just in time to help save the day. Believing they are failures, Mujab and Samir are surprised when they are hailed as heroes by the townspeople because they came back to stand up to the bandits, and that took courage.

Story Lessons
- Encourage children to be honest and to avoid the temptation to tell lies in order to impress others.
- Help children understand that when they pretend to be someone they are not, this usually leads to negative consequences and can hurt others around them.
- Teach children that lies never last. Eventually, they catch up to you.

CLASS PLAN

Pre-Viewing Activity (Approximately 5 Minutes)

Have a discussion about what motivates people to tell lies. Sometimes the reason is to get a reward (example: a child might lie about their accomplishments to impress friends). Other times, people tell lies to avoid punishment (example: a child says they didn't break an object in their home). As they watch the episode or listen to the story, have students look for how telling lies gets the characters in big trouble, and presents problems for others in the community.

Watch or Read Episode (Approximately 10 Minutes)

Post-Viewing Discussion Questions (Approximately 10 Minutes)

What lessons do Mujab and Samir learn in this story?
(*Discussion:* First, lying about who you are never lasts. They learned that when they pretended to be people they were not (lawmen), other people eventually found out the truth. Second, lying can have consequences and hurt others. In this case, Mujab and Samir lied about being lawmen, and because the town was relying on them to fend off criminals, their lie put the town at risk. Lying was not only bad, because they got caught, but it also put the town's safety in jeopardy.)

Why do the townspeople consider Mujab and Samir heroes at the end?
(*Discussion:* Even though Mujab and Samir were not lawmen, they bravely returned to the town and did their best to right their wrong. They also knew that standing up to the criminals would probably result in serious harm to them, but they did it because they felt they owed it to the town, and that took courage.)

What do you think would have happened if the real lawman didn't show up at the end?
(*Discussion:* Mujab and Samir would have been hurt, and the bandits probably would have robbed more and caused more trouble in the community. This illustrates that telling lies can have serious consequences.)

In-Class Activity – for 50-60 Minute Lessons (Approximately 30 Minutes)

To help students explore the consequences that happen when someone tries to deceive others, present these two examples. In each, the character confides that he or she told a lie and naively wonders, *What could possibly go wrong?*

Example 1: Hi, my name is Hussein, and I have a big math test tomorrow. But I LOVE football. Instead of spending the afternoon studying for the test, I played football outside. I told my parents I had finished my homework in school. Not true! But, hey, it was such a beautiful day, and I really wanted to spend time with my friends. **What could possibly go wrong?**

Example 2: Hi, I'm Zahra. When I went to the store today to buy a book, the cashier made a mistake and gave me too much change. Can you believe my good luck? I probably should go back to the store to report the mistake, but then I would have to give back the money. **What could possibly go wrong?**

Divide students into pairs and have them discuss both situations and the consequences of different actions. Why do they think the person told a lie or did not tell the truth? Have each pair come up with three reasons why the person in the example should not have lied or should have been honest.

Afterward, have all the pairs share their discussions with the whole class. Talk about all the consequences of lying. Remind them that it is not just about avoiding punishment. In the first example, the student would not only get a poor grade, but he would also not master important math concepts that would help them on future tests (and even later in life). In the second example, the cashier might be fired for the money error, or the student might eventually get caught. Additionally, they are creating a society where lying and cheating are okay.

ACTIVITY ONE: WHY LYING IS A BAD IDEA

Telling lies might seem like a smart decision. Sometimes lies can lead to getting rewards or avoiding punishment. But these consequences are short-lived. Eventually, lies lead to more lies, and, ultimately, to the liar getting caught.

Hamid wants to play with his friends, but his mother said he can't play until his homework is done. Hamid is thinking of lying and telling her that his work is done, so he can go out and play. *Give Hamid five reasons why lying is not a very good idea.* We've started by giving you two.

1. Lying is wrong. You don't want people to lie to you, so you shouldn't lie to others.

2. Hamid's mother could find out the truth, and then he'll get into trouble.

3. _____
   _____

4. _____
   _____

5. _____
   _____

TAKE-HOME ACTIVITY

NAME: _____

THE FORBIDDEN CITY OF SHENZHEN

Story Summary

Shahryar is informed by Ambassador Kadeer that Prince Lufti heard from King Fawwaz that King Siamak told him that Shahryar has a bad temper. Shahryar can't believe someone would say this and is furious, threatening war. Shahrzad explains to Shahryar that listening to rumors can often lead to misunderstandings. She tells him this story:

A curious boy named Anming ventures where he's not supposed to and falls down a steep wall into the forbidden city of Shenzhen. The people of Anming's village fear the inhabitants of Shenzhen because they have heard about their primitive and barbaric ways. Anming makes friends with the people of Shenzhen and learns they aren't primitive or barbaric at all; they're just like the people from his village. When the villagers come to rescue Anming, both sides are about to go to war. Anming comes between them and stops them, showing them that their perceptions of each other are based on complete misunderstandings. In truth, neither side is primitive or barbaric. In the end, they all become friends and learn to live together peacefully.

Story Lessons

- Encourage children to be curious about and to appreciate differences in other cultures. Help them realize that all people deserve respect and have many positive qualities in common.
- Help children understand that prejudices are often based on irrational beliefs that date back many years and that first-hand experience is often a powerful antidote to combat prejudice and misunderstandings. Don't believe everything you hear until you can prove it yourself.
- Encourage children to speak up when they hear someone say something offensive or untrue about another person or group of people.

CLASS PLAN

Pre-Viewing Activity (Approximately 5 Minutes)

Have a brief discussion of what a misunderstanding is. To help get students thinking about how misunderstandings can lead to problems, share a personal story about a rumor that wasn't true. Maybe someone jumped to the wrong conclusion based on a superficial detail. For example, a student football player once went to the school doctor because his leg hurt. Rumors quickly spread that the student's leg was paralyzed and that he would never play football again. It turned out that the leg injury was merely a bad cramp that went away in a matter of minutes.

Watch or Read Episode (Approximately 10 Minutes)

Post-Viewing Discussion Questions (Approximately 10 Minutes)

What are some of the rumors that Anming hears about the people of Shenzhen? Where did these rumors come from? What is the truth about these rumors?
(*Discussion:* Anming has heard that the people of Shenzhen boil one another in big pots, hammer nails into their bodies, and eat worms. The truth is that these people take warm baths in big tubs, practice acupuncture, and eat noodles.)

At the end of the story, Shahrzad said it showed that ignorance breeds fear. How does not knowing about someone else lead to being afraid of them?
(*Discussion:* Not knowing about someone else can cause you to imagine the worst about him or her.)

What should you do if you hear a rumor about one of your friends?
(*Discussion:* If you have proof that the rumor is not true, you shouldn't repeat it. You may also dispute it to the person who told you about it.)

What should you do if you hear people make assumptions about other groups of people?
(*Discussion:* You should always question negative assumptions about other people. If someone says "Those people are bad" or "Those people don't like us," you should always ask why and try to figure out if that makes sense or if you have things in common with the other people that can help overcome your differences.)

In-Class Activity – for 50-60 Minute Lessons (Approximately 30 Minutes)

Children often base their relationships on first impressions rather than real information. Write these three questions on the board: What is your favorite food? What is a food you don't like? What is something you like to talk about? Have students write their responses on a piece of paper—but not put their names on it. Collect all the papers, shuffle them, and then hand them out randomly, one to each student. The goal is for the student to get a response from a different student (if he or she gets his or her own, have them switch with another student's paper). Ask each student to look at the three responses written down and ask themselves: *Do I think this person and I might have a fun lunch together? Why or why not?* Then reveal the identities of the writers. How many surprises did you find? Are you friends with the writer? Why or why not? If not, do you have something in common that could help you build a friendship with the writer?

ACTIVITY ONE: SPEAK UP!

How come King Nihar never visits my castle? What's wrong with him? He seemed like a nice guy the one time we met. Doesn't he like the food we serve or the games we play?

How come King Shahryar never invites me to his castle? I would love to visit, but he never sends me an invitation. Maybe he doesn't like the way I dress? Or thinks that his food is too good for me?

Directions: Imagine that you could get both kings in the same room for a few minutes. What would you say to each of them to help them get along and to realize their misunderstandings? Write down three things you would say to them below.

1. _____

2. _____

3. _____

TAKE-HOME ACTIVITY

NAME: _____

THE BROKEN JEWEL

Note: Activity One can work either as a complement to the In-Class Activity, or can be given as a Take-Home Activity.

Story Summary

When Shahryar is petrified to see a dentist, Shahrzad tells him that when you face your fears, you often find out they are not as bad as you think. She tells him this story:

Two servants, Mustaf and Asad, accidentally break a jewel in the king's crown. It turns out the jewel is a rare crystal that can only be found at the top of a huge mountain. Instead of telling the king their mistake, they embark on a treacherous journey up the mountain to find a crystal like the one they broke. They barely escape with their lives and return with a replacement. Unfortunately, when they are replacing it in the crown, the replacement crystal drops and breaks. While they react in horror, the king walks in, forcing them to confess. Unfazed, the king tells them to be more careful and then opens a drawerful of similar crystals and places a new one in the crown. Mustaf and Asad realize they climbed the mountain for nothing. If they had been brave and simply told the king the truth right away, they wouldn't have had to endure all those hardships.

Story Lessons
- Encourage children to take responsibility for their actions, and to tell the truth, even when the consequences could be dire.
- Encourage children to face their fears and to realize that the fear of doing something is often worse than actually doing it.

CLASS PLAN

Pre-Viewing Activity (Approximately 5 Minutes)

Everyone makes mistakes. How they respond to their mistakes separates those individuals with integrity and character from those who lack these qualities. Some people make mistakes and then try to hide them from others. Other people not only admit their mistakes, but also take steps to right them. Ask: Can you think of any examples of each kind? After encouraging an open-ended discussion, provide an example or two. Imagine Person B borrows a toy from Person A. Person B accidentally breaks a part of the toy. What are some different things Person B could do or not do? What would be the consequences of doing each option? What should Person B do?

Explain that in today's story they are about to see/hear, the characters are faced with a similar dilemma. They wonder if they should hide their error or admit the truth.

Watch or Read Episode (Approximately 10 Minutes)

Post-Viewing Discussion Questions (Approximately 10 Minutes)

Why doesn't Shahryar want to tell others that he is afraid of going to the dentist?
(*Discussion:* Shahryar is worried that the others will think less of him if he admits his fear. He mistakenly believes that he shouldn't be afraid of anything. He doesn't realize that fear is a natural reaction, and that every person has fears.)

When Asad and Mustaf break the king's jewel, Asad says, "No one's going to find out." If you did something wrong, and were absolutely sure that no one would find out, would you admit the truth? Why or why not?
(*Discussion:* Telling the truth is the right thing to do, for oneself as well as one's community. Everyone makes mistakes. By admitting your failures, you can show responsibility to others and reveal how grown up you are. Telling lies also leads to more deception, which can make things worse because people won't trust you anymore.)

What if Asad and Mustaf had admitted the truth when they first broke the jewel? How would their experience have been different?
(*Discussion:* These men would not have had to travel to the top of the dangerous mountain to find a replacement jewel. The King would have accepted their honest apology, and they would have continued on with their lives.)

Some people mistakenly believe that brave people don't have any fears. In truth, everyone has some fears. It's just that the brave people act despite their fears. What are some ways to encourage oneself or a friend to act bravely?
(*Discussion:* There are some physical things you can do to fight the anxiety or fear, such as taking deep breaths – slowly in through the nose to the count of five; then breath out through your mouth to the count of five.)

In-Class Activity – for 50-60 Minute Lessons (Approximately 30 Minutes)

Ask students what it means to be a responsible person. Have them list some of the qualities of such a person (trustworthy, takes responsibility, etc.).

Learning to apologize for doing something wrong or hurtful can be very difficult for children (and many adults)! But part of being responsible for one's actions is learning this important skill. One effective way to apologize is to write a letter. Have students think of someone to whom they could write an apology letter. The goal is for each student to write a letter saying they are sorry for the action they took—and would like to try to make it up to the other person. Sometimes by putting words in a letter, a person can better organize his or her thoughts and give the reader a chance to think about what is written. The reasons for the apology can be minor. For example, the student could apologize to a parent for forgetting to pick up their dirty laundry off the floor of his or her room or for not completing a household chore. Another example could be offering an apology to someone for losing his or her temper.

Directions: Apologizing for doing something wrong isn't easy, but it is the right thing to do. Just ask Asad and Mustaf! But learning to tell someone else you feel sorry is a big part of growing up and being responsible. Use this page to write an apology letter to a friend or family member. You don't have to show it to anyone else in class. Some people find it helpful to write down notes for their letter on a separate page before actually writing the letter.

Dear _____ ,

In school, we have been learning about different ways of being more responsible. One way is to apologize for doing something wrong or hurtful. That is why I am writing to you. I wanted to say that I'm very sorry for

_____

_____

How can I make it up to you? How about if I

_____

_____

Thanks for taking the time to read this note.

From,

_____

TAKE-HOME ACTIVITY

NAME: _____

ACTIVITY TWO: FACE A FEAR TOGETHER   LESSON TWENTY SIX

Directions: Do this activity at home with a parent or other adult family member.

It is natural to feel afraid sometimes. If you accidentally fell from a high place, you'd naturally feel scared of heights. But there are other times when you might feel very scared about something that isn't as dangerous — such as being alone in the dark in a safe place, talking in front of a group of adults, or meeting new people and hoping to fit in.

With help from an adult, write down one thing that you wish you were less afraid of: _____

Write how being afraid of this thing/situation gets in the way of your happiness   _____
(and being a better member of your community):   _____

What can you do to face and overcome your fear?:   _____
          _____

Here are some ways that other children have gotten over their fears.

Some Techniques For Overcoming Fears:

- Deep breathing
- Exercise (running, jumping jacks etc.)
- Muscle tensing / relaxing
- Talking with others (sharing feelings, worries)
- Thinking about something else for a while
- Imagining "worst case scenario" and trying to see the unlikelihood of it
- Imagining "best case scenario" and focusing on that instead of what could go wrong
- Trying something similar but less scary and working your way up to the thing that's scary (example: talking to a small group of close friends or family members before trying to speak in front of your entire school)
- Laughing - finding the humor in one's fear
- Music (listening to inspirational music; singing songs)

TAKE-HOME ACTIVITY   NAME: _____

THE BOY WHO BECAME A GENIE

Story Summary

When Shahzaman wishes that he were a gladiator instead of having to study in school, Shahrzad warns him to be careful what he wishes for. She tells him the story of a boy who wished for a different life, and it didn't turn out too well:

A boy named Harif finds a bottle with a genie inside and makes a wish that they trade places. The boy becomes the genie, and the genie becomes the boy. Later, when Harif wants to switch back, the genie refuses. Harif is now trapped forever as a genie inside a bottle. With the help of his sister and his faithful dog, he outsmarts the genie and returns to his old self. He learns his lesson, though – be careful what you wish for. A wild dream might not be all that you hoped it would be.

Story Lessons
- Encourage children to appreciate everything they already have, especially their family. It is sometimes easy to envy what we don't have rather than appreciate what we do have.
- Remind children that everything has good sides and bad sides to it. If some of their wishes were to come true, these wishes would come with unexpected consequences.

CLASS PLAN

Pre-Viewing Activity (Approximately 5 Minutes)

Introduce this story about genies by having students imagine that a genie granted them one wish that would enable them to change one thing about themselves. This magical change would last forever. Have students write down their wish anonymously on a piece of paper and place it into a box. Each student picks out one of the wishes (not his or her own), and says two things about that wish: (1) something good that might come from that wish and (2) something bad that might come from that wish. This could lead to a discussion about how choices we make sometimes have unintended consequences.

Watch or Read Episode (Approximately 10 Minutes)

Post-Viewing Discussion Questions (Approximately 10 Minutes)

The genie tricked Harif. Do you think this was right or wrong? Why?
(*Discussion:* The genie's treatment of Harif was unfair and wrong. He took advantage of Harif's frustration and didn't tell Harif the whole story. It was wrong of the genie to trap Harif in the bottle.)

Imagine that you trade something with another person, but then the person has second thoughts and asks you to trade back. How do you feel? What should you do? What if you tricked the other person and didn't tell them the whole truth?
(*Discussion:* Students' answers will vary. Many children will feel cheated and upset by the person going back on their trade. In this situation, children could say that a "trade is a trade" and stick with the arrangement, OR they could agree to reverse the trade, if they feel it is reasonable or they feel the other party didn't realize everything they were getting when they made the trade decision.)

Why did the genie want to switch places with Harif?
(*Discussion:* The genie felt that freedom was more important than all the power in the world.)

Why did the boy, Harif, want to switch places with the genie? Why did he regret this decision after it happened?
(*Discussion:* The boy thought about all of the wonderful things he'd gain by becoming a genie, but he didn't think about what he'd have to give up, and the genie didn't tell him. The genie told him he could have everything and then trapped him in a bottle and took away his freedom.)

How did Harif feel when he realized he could not go back to being himself?
(*Discussion:* Harif felt angry and trapped. Because Harif only looked at the benefits of becoming a genie, he didn't see the flip side. Students will probably comment that the genie's tricking Harif was unfair. Harif was not allowed to reverse his decision once he realized it was a poor one that kept him away from his family.)

In-Class Activity – for 50-60 Minute Lessons (Approximately 30 Minutes)

In this episode, the genie tricks Harif into switching places and then forces him to stay in this situation forever. The genie is completely inflexible, even when the boy pleads that they go back to their original lives. To help students explore what this might feel like, and to help emphasize that there are usually good and bad sides to every choice, have them work with a partner to explore this question: If you could change places with the genie, would you, and why or why not? If you could, would you switch places with anyone else in the world? If so, who would you pick and why?

Have the partner help the person examine all the positive aspects of this switch and help point out some of the problems that would be raised by it. It is important to emphasize that, like in this story, this switch is permanent. What would they miss about their old life?

Genies can be trapped in their bottles for a long time (sometimes hundreds of years)! If a genie asked you to change places with him, like Harif did, would you do it? Why or why not? Write your answer to the genie below.

Dear Genie,

I've thought about your offer to change places with me and have decided

_____

_____

_____

_____

_____

_____

_____

_____

_____

_____

ACTIVITY TWO: BEWARE! THE POWER OF ADVERTISING!

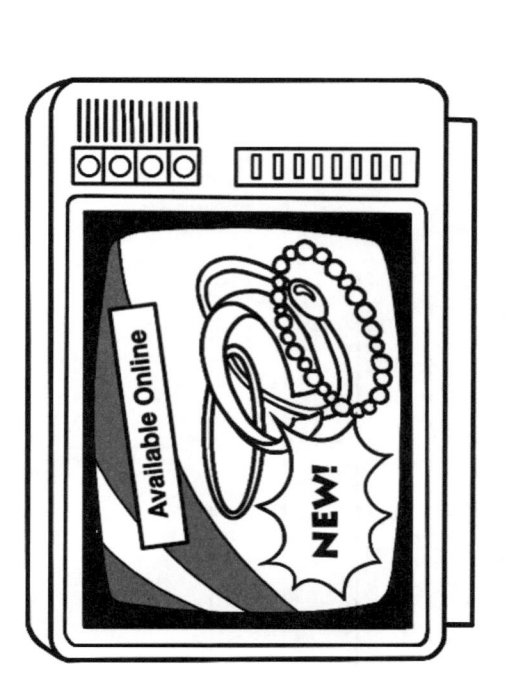

Many advertisements in newspapers or on TV try to convince you to buy something you don't really need. These advertisements often do a great job telling you all the benefits of a new product but avoid telling you about all the downsides. Why do you think they do this? _____

Work with a family member to find some advertisements and then talk about how the people who made them tried to persuade you to buy it. You might choose an ad for a food you buy or a toy that a company wants children to ask their parents for.

NAME OF PRODUCT: _____

WAYS THE PRODUCT IS SUPPOSED TO IMPROVE YOUR LIFE: _____

POSSIBLE PROBLEMS WITH THIS PRODUCT: _____

IF SOMEONE GAVE YOU THE MONEY TO BUY THIS PROJECT, WOULD YOU? _____

WHY OR WHY NOT? _____

TAKE-HOME ACTIVITY

NAME: _____

THE TALE OF THE MOUNTAIN AND THE VALLEY

Note: Prior to class, teachers of the 50-60 minute class, will need to make multiple copies of Activity Sheet One for the In-Class Activity.

Story Summary

A simple misunderstanding gets blown out of proportion when Shahryar tells Shahrzad that he isn't feeling well. Shahrzad tells Donyazad that he's sick and won't be coming to dinner. Donyazad tells Shahzaman that Shahryar doesn't want to eat Rajani's food because he's sick. Shahzaman tells Rajani that his food makes Shahryar sick. Rajani is now upset and thinks he's going to be fired. When Shahrzad realizes the misunderstanding, she tells the kids the following story about some people who lived on top of a mountain who almost went to war with the people who lived in the valley below them, and all because of a silly misunderstanding:

Two tourists ask the proprietor of a teahouse which trail to take to get to the top of the mountain. When the tourists leave, the proprietor tells one of his customers that the people who came in must be mountain people. Another customer says the people who live on top of the mountain are thieves. This starts a conversation within the valley about mountain people and each time the information is passed on, another misunderstanding occurs. Soon the valley people are talking about how the mountain people are coming down into the valley and stealing things. Dealing with the hysteria, the mayor of the valley posts guards to protect the town. Unfortunately, when the mountain people see the guards, they think the valley people are mobilizing their army for an attack. In response, they mobilize their army. When the valley people see this, their concerns were verified and they now know the mountain people are about to attack. Both sides meet on the battlefield, only to learn that neither side is planning an attack. They laugh at the misunderstanding and return to their normal lives.

Story Lessons

- Encourage children to be respectful and tolerant of others who are different and to avoid misunderstandings by not jumping to conclusions about others' actions and intentions.
- Encourage children not to believe rumors and to understand the potential dangers of gossip. When people spread rumors, this often leads to trouble and hurt feelings.
- Help children understand that violence begets violence, but problems can be solved when calm heads prevail.

CLASS PLAN

Pre-Viewing Activity (Approximately 5 Minutes)

Introduce the theme of miscommunication by playing the classic telephone game. Students sit in a circle, and the teacher whispers a few detailed sentences into the ear of the student next to him or her. Example: *"A large man came to the palace and greeted the king with a monkey on his shoulder. The king was happy and said, 'I like your monkey.' Please stay for dinner."* Then the student whispers what he or she thinks he or she heard into the ear of the student next to him or her (but may only whisper it once). This continues around the circle, with each student whispering what he or she thinks is the message until it reaches the last student. The last student says his or her version of the message aloud. The teacher tells the group what the original message was.

Important: The teacher should make sure that all the laughter at the misunderstandings is good-natured – and point out that everyone can make mistakes when hearing detailed information.

Have a discussion about how messages sometimes change as they move from person to person. As students watch/ listen to the story about the mountain and the valley, have them look for examples of when people are spreading rumors and gossip. What do they think the people should have done instead?

Watch or Read Episode (Approximately 10 Minutes)

Post-Viewing Discussion Questions (Approximately 10 Minutes)

What is a misunderstanding? What are some examples from this story?
(*Discussion:* A misunderstanding is an idea that someone has that isn't based on facts. Someone hears only part of the story, or someone exaggerates a detail, and this leads someone else to jump to conclusions. There are many examples of misunderstandings in this story. For example, when the mayor of the valley posts guards to protect the town, the mountain people see the guards and think that the valley people are getting ready for an attack.)

Why does Rajani the chef think that Shahryar hates his cooking? Did Shahryar really hate his cooking? How could this rumor have been stopped much earlier?
(*Discussion:* What really happened was Shahryar was feeling ill, so he requested not to have dinner that night. When this message was spread from person to person, the result was that Rajani heard the message that Shahryar was sick of his cooking. This caused Rajani to worry that he would be fired from his job. If each person who spread the message had been more careful about listening and speaking, then the message would have reached Rajani more accurately.)

What does it feel like to have someone say mean things about you?
(*Discussion:* Having others spread rumors and gossip about you is hurtful, and it makes you feel angry at those who did so.)

In-Class Activity – for 50-60 Minute Lessons (Approximately 30 Minutes)

Lead students through the activity on Activity Sheet One. In this activity, all students look at the same detailed picture and write about what they see. Afterward, students share their writing and will discover that different people focused on different aspects of the picture and that people sometimes jumped to conclusions about what was going on.

ACTIVITY ONE: SAME PICTURE, DIFFERENT STORIES

Directions: Look at this detailed picture and then write a paragraph about what you think is going on. There are no right answers. You might focus on one part of the picture, and a classmate might focus on another. The important thing is to work independently. THEN, after everyone is done, have each (or a few students) read their paragraph aloud. Discuss why you think each person came away with a different story about the same picture.

TAKE-HOME ACTIVITY

NAME: _____

ACTIVITY TWO: STOP THE RUMOR

Spreading rumors can be hurtful. A rumor is a piece of information that may or may not be true and spreading them about others is wrong. You have the power to stop rumors from spreading. What can you do?

WAYS TO STOP RUMORS FROM SPREADING

1. Decide that you're not going to let the rumor spread anymore. You could say, "Sorry, I don't spread rumors. That's mean" or "You wouldn't like it if someone spread a rumor about you."

2. Tell a parent, teacher, or other grown-up that you've heard a rumor and are concerned. (If you need to tell the adult the rumor, make sure to do it privately, so no one else will hear.)

3. Create a poster for your classroom or school hallway that reminds others that spreading rumors can hurt people's feelings.

WHAT OTHER IDEAS DO YOU HAVE?

4. _____

_____

5. _____

_____

6. _____

_____

TAKE-HOME ACTIVITY

NAME: _____

Guess what I just heard....

BIGGER, BADDER, BADR

Story Summary

Shahryar is furious when he sees a puppet show that makes fun of the king. He's about to pass a law that makes it illegal to mock him when Shahrzad reminds him that a sense of humor is a good thing. A strong king isn't afraid of criticism. She tells him this story:

There was a king named Badr who was cruel and heartless to his people. A peasant named Faruq goes to him and asks him to make some changes. Badr refuses and throws Faruq out, so Faruq leads a protest of townspeople to ask for changes. "What can the king do?" asks Faruq. "He can't throw us all in prison." The next day, they're all in prison. Badr then forces them to work as slaves in the salt mines. Faruq convinces everyone to refuse to work. "We're already in prison!" he shouts to them. "What more can he do to us?" The next day, they're standing in the arena, about to be eaten by lions. They manage to escape, but Badr orders them rounded up and brought to him. When the soldiers go to the peasants' homes, however, they find that everyone has moved away; none of them want to live in this kingdom anymore. Soon the soldiers leave too, and Badr is the only one left in the kingdom. He tried to say that he's sorry, but it's too late. He's now forever the king of nothing.

Story Lessons
- Help children understand that effective leaders should have a sense of humor and feel secure enough to handle the concerns and criticisms of their constituents. The role of a leader of people is to govern for the benefit of the people and in accordance with how the people want to be led/governed. The ability to speak freely is important, because the people need to be able to express how they feel.
- Inspire children to see that when groups of like-minded people work together, they can achieve change peacefully.

CLASS PLAN

Pre-Viewing Activity (Approximately 5 Minutes)

Imagine that your school decides that comic books are no longer allowed in school. You and your friends love comic books, and sometimes they can be educational. What can you and your friends do to respectfully address this issue with your teachers and the school? If ideas are brought up respectfully, how should the teachers and school respond?

Tell the students they are about to watch or hear a story about King Badr and someone who wanted changes in his kingdom.

Watch or Read Episode (Approximately 10 Minutes)

Post-Viewing Discussion Questions (Approximately 10 Minutes)

Do you think Faruq's requests to King Badr were reasonable?
(*Discussion:* Students' opinions will vary. Faruq had asked the king if he could reduce the taxes, have his subjects work shorter days, and not have as strict punishments for minor crimes. Many students might find these requests reasonable.)

Why is it useful for a leader to be comfortable with hearing criticism about him- or herself?
(*Discussion:* No one is perfect. A smart leader realizes that good ideas can come from anywhere, and some of these good ideas involve changing his or her attitudes or behaviors. Wise leaders are open to new ideas and appreciate positive feedback from those who live in his or her society.)

When Faruq comes up against resistance by the king, he becomes "more determined than ever." Why do you think Faruq is so determined?
(*Discussion:* Faruq persists because he strongly believes that his requests are fair and reasonable. He also believes that if he speaks his mind honestly and respectfully, then others in the community will follow and support him.)

What is "freedom of speech"? Why is this concept useful to a society?
(*Discussion:* Freedom of speech means that people who live in a society are free to speak their minds and to have a respectful dialogue with their leader without fear of being punished. The leader is not obligated to give the people what they ask for, but he or she needs to show the community that he or she is open to hearing their ideas.)

In-Class Activity – for 50-60 Minute Lessons (Approximately 30 Minutes)

Divide students into small groups. Each group's mission is to come up with a proposal for a change they would like to see in their classroom. It is important that this change be reasonable. Discuss what reasonable means – and give examples that support the teacher's philosophy and style. For instance, a group might propose that they be able to decorate the classroom, have a different seating arrangement, or change their morning recess to an afternoon recess.

Each group has to come up with a one-to-two-minute presentation of their proposal. They can use visuals (a list of benefits, for example). The teacher says that as long as there is a reasonable suggestion, he or she will pick one of the groups' proposals and implement it for a short period of time, as an experiment. If it is successful, then the group's proposal might become a permanent part of the class's policies.

Directions: With a family member, talk about the different ways that people make changes in your community or country. Read a newspaper or magazine together and find an example of an ordinary citizen taking action to help others. For example, it could be a new policy that keeps children safer at school. Fill in the page below and tell us who you admire and why.

Name of person:

_____

What action did they take?

_____

_____

_____

Why was this action extraordinary?

_____

_____

_____

Three things I can do to make this happen:

1. _____

2. _____

3. _____

Did you know that you have the power to change the world? I'm not kidding. Every little positive change that you make in your life, and in the lives of others, makes the world a little better. Sometimes a LOT better!

What I would like to change:

_____

_____

_____

_____

Think of something you'd like to change in your home or neighborhood. How might you go about making that happen?

THE RIDDLE OF THE RUINED TOMB

Note: Prior to class, teachers will need to make multiple copies of the Pre-Viewing Activity Sheet, which is attached at the back of this lesson plan.

Story Summary

Shahryar, Shahzaman, and Donyazad all see something different when they look at the same painting. Shahrzad tells them that what you see depends on your point of view. She tells them this story:

On a stormy night in ancient Persia, a man named Nayzar looks out his window and thinks he sees another man named Hamed chop down a tree, which lands on the famous Tomb of Avicenna and destroys it. However, Nayzar is contradicted by two women who both say they saw the tree standing an hour after Nayzar claimed he saw Hamed cut it down. Hamed denies chopping the tree down altogether. With so many different accounts by different people, no one can figure out what really happened. In the end, they find out that each person's account of what they witnessed was only part of what actually happened. They learn that even when things seem obviously true, the way you see things sometimes depends on your point of view.

Story Lessons

- Encourage children to realize that people have different perspectives. To uncover the whole truth, one has to consider more than one point of view.
- Help children understand that circumstantial evidence is not enough to prove someone guilty of a crime.

CLASS PLAN

Pre-Viewing Activity (Approximately 5 Minutes)

To get students thinking about different points of view, have children look at the optical illusion (provided on the last page of this lesson plan) for ten seconds, then write down a short answer to: What do you see in this picture?

Students can share their observations, then have a discussion about how the truth is sometimes more complicated than it appears. More than one answer can be right, depending on your point of view.

Watch or Read Episode (Approximately 10 Minutes)

Post-Viewing Discussion Questions (Approximately 10 Minutes)

Why does everyone in town think Hamed chopped down the tree that fell on the tomb?
(*Discussion:* The townspeople only listened to the account of one person, Nayzar, who looked out of his window and saw Hamed with an ax, chopping. He didn't know the whole story: Hamed was actually chasing an aggressive snake that had entered Hamed's home and was threatening to eat his pet bird.)

In this story, different people saw things that seemed to contradict one another. Is it possible for two people to see events that contradict one another and both be right? What should you do when you believe something to be different than someone else?
(*Discussion:* Two people can see things that seem to contradict one another and both can be right. When you believe something different from someone else, it is important to respect the other person's opinion and understand that both of you can be right. You should first respect one another's opinions and beliefs and then try to calmly investigate the facts. If you still find that you disagree, understand that you both can still be correct while believing different things.)

If you were accused of something you didn't do, what could you do to help others find out the truth?
(*Discussion:* You could tell the truth from your point of view, look for other people who can confirm your story or who know what really happened, or try to figure out alternative explanations for what happened. You could put yourself in his or her shoes and try to think why they thought the way they did.)

Why is it important to look at all the facts before you accuse someone of doing something wrong?
(*Discussion:* It is important to gather as much evidence as possible, because appearances can be deceiving. If you only know about part of what happened, then your perspective will be skewed and you will be more likely to jump to false conclusions.)

In-Class Activity – for 50-60 Minute Lessons (Approximately 30 Minutes)

To help students explore the concept of seeing an object or situation from different points of view, begin by telling them the following story:

There was once a group of five blind men who walked through a forest. On one fine day, they came across an animal whose sound they associated with that of an elephant. Being blind, they had never seen an elephant before and all were curious to know what this elephant looks like, how big it was, what its skin feels like, and how much it weighed. Curious and excited, they all approached the elephant and touched it.

The first of the blind men touched its tusk and declared, "The elephant is a thin creature with a hard, bonelike exterior and pointy, sharp ends."

The second blind man, who happened to touch the elephant's trunk, said, "I am not sure I agree with you, sahib. The elephant is long, slender, and strong, but it has a soft exterior that is smooth, and his body is very flexible."

The third blind man, who happened to grab the tail, was very confused. He said, "My dear friends, I don't know if your hands deceive you, but the elephant is long and very thin, with hair. This animal is as light as a feather, not very strong, and its movements are fast and wispy!"

The fourth man wrapped his arms around one leg of the beast and said, "Sahibs, this animal is not hairy, and it is certainly not light and wispy. I can wrap my arms around its entire body, but I am pushing and pulling, and this animal will not budge!"

The fifth man walked forward and touched the large body of the elephant. "My dear friends", he said, "You are all wrong, or we are touching different animals entirely. The animal before me has no part that I would call hard, pointy, or bony. It has no hair, is not slender or long. It is certainly not light, thin, slender, or wispy, and there is no way to put your arms around any part of this creature. This animal is huge and could crush us all if it did not float suspended in the air."

Which of the blind men was correct? Were all of them right? Were all of them wrong? Explain to the students that all were right in part, but each had a different perspective based on their experience and point of view. It would be wrong to conclude that one was right or wrong. Collectively, they would understand the elephant much more and better if they respected one another's opinions.

Divide the class into three groups. Each group is given one observation and ten minutes to brainstorm different explanations of what is going on. Each group should then present the possibilities to the rest of the class.

Observations:

1. You witness someone taking a book from the teacher's desk when nobody is looking.
2. You are walking home from school, and you see someone climbing in the window of a house.
3. On your way home from school, you see your neighbor coming toward you with fresh flowers, and when you get to your house, you notice flowers are missing from your garden.

What are the possible outcomes for each of these observations?

With a family member's help, write a true story about a time when someone thought you did something wrong, but you did not. Tell how the experience felt. Here are some questions to help you think about your story:

What did people **think** happened? _____
_____
_____
_____
_____
_____
_____

What **really** happened? _____
_____
_____
_____
_____
_____

How did it feel to have people have the wrong idea? _____
_____
_____
_____

How did it feel once they knew the truth (assuming they did)?
_____
_____
_____
_____

Additional questions to consider:

Why is it important to gather all the facts before you accuse someone of wrongdoing? _____
_____

If someone is wrongly accused, what are some strategies you could use to convince others of what really happened?

_____
_____

TAKE-HOME ACTIVITY

NAME: _____

PRE-VIEWING ACTIVITY: WHAT IS THIS A PICTURE OF?

NAME: _____

THE MERCHANT AND THE PICKPOCKET

Story Summary

Shahryar mistakes a visiting king for a beggar and orders Majid to get rid of him. Shahrzad tells him this story about prejudging people:

A young thief named Adnaan is caught trying to pickpocket two wealthy gentlemen, Karthik and Bharat. Karthik wants the boy arrested, but Bharat gives Adnaan money to get his shoes from the repair shop. Karthik thinks Bharat is insane, insisting that the boy is bad and will run off with the money. Bharat bets him the boy will return. Adnaan does run off with the money and spends part of it with his friend, another young thief named Naresh. Karthik tracks down Adnaan and brings him to Bharat to return the money. When Adnaan opens the moneybag, he realizes that Naresh stole the money from him. Karthik doesn't believe the boy and wants him arrested, but Bharat lets him go. Adnaan fights Naresh to retrieve the stolen money, and returns it to Bharat, along with his shoes from the repair shop. Bharat wins his bet. When Karthik asks him how he knew the boy would do the right thing, Bharat explains that he also grew up a thief on those streets, and someone once gave him a second chance, which helped him become who he is today. Karthik learns that one should never judge a book by its cover, and the importance of giving someone a second chance.

Story Lessons
- Inspire children to act compassionately toward others and to try to understand what it might feel like to be in someone else's shoes.
- Help children understand that it is not right to prejudge people based on their appearances.
- Encourage children to realize that nobody is inherently bad. Some people make bad choices partly due to difficult circumstances, and varying degrees of luck/opportunity.
- Inspire children to understand that everyone has the ability to improve their behavior. Everyone deserves a second chance.

CLASS PLAN

Pre-Viewing Activity (Approximately 5 Minutes)

Ask: Do you believe that everyone deserves a second chance? Why or why not? Point out that no one is perfect. We all make mistakes. How we respond to others says a lot about who we are. We should try to act toward others the way we'd like others to act toward us.

Imagine that you are the owner of a supermarket. You see a poor, hungry man try to steal a pack of biscuits or fruit by putting it inside his coat. As he leaves the store, you approach him. What should you do? Have students brainstorm some options. You might have him arrested? Or you might ask him why he stole from you? Or you might offer him a job in your store, in exchange for food. Discuss which option is the most compassionate. Which option is the least compassionate? Which approach do you think would make the hungry man less likely to steal from the store in the future?

Can you think of other examples from your life when you gave someone a second chance, or a time when someone gave you a second chance? Tell them they are about to watch an episode (or hear a story) about second chances.

Watch or Read Episode (Approximately 10 Minutes)

Post-Viewing Discussion Questions (Approximately 10 Minutes)

Adnaan had a poor upbringing and lived on the street. Did this make it okay for him to steal? Was Kharthik right when he wanted to call the police? Why did Bharat decide to not call the police?
(*Discussion:* We should feel sorry for Adnaan, because he was poor and had a bad upbringing. Stealing, however, is wrong. Bharat knows that Adnaan stole, and that this is wrong, but instead of judging him, Bharat thought he could be understanding and help him. Both Karthik and Bharat were right and neither was wrong in how they reacted, however their approaches were different.)

Do you think it was a wise decision for the wealthy man (Bharat) to trust the boy (Adnaan) with the bag of money to pick up his (Bharat's) shoes? Why or why not? If you were in Bharat's place, what would you have done?
(*Discussion:* It depends. Bharat's decision to trust Adnaan turned out to be a good one, but there was no guarantee that it would have worked out that way. Bharat took a risk, and he might have lost his money. But if Bharat had not trusted Adnaan, then Adnaan would never have had the opportunity to show others (and himself) that he could be a trustworthy person.)

When one of the wealthy men catches the boys stealing, he says, "Kids like him are no good!" Do you agree with him? Why or why not? Do you think that criminals can change, or are they locked into that way of behaving forever?
(*Discussion:* As this story argues, prejudging a person, based on their appearances, is wrong. Sometimes people make poor choices based on circumstances beyond their control, or simply bad luck. Remember that people have the ability to improve their lives—but they have to want to make these changes, and it sometimes takes a lot of hard work and the support of friends.)

In-Class Activity – for 50-60 Minute Lessons (Approximately 30 Minutes)

To help students explore the topic of empathy, and imagine life in someone else's shoes, do the following activity. Draw the following series of five to six life-size footprints on pieces of paper and place them on the ground. Label each set of footprints accordingly:

- Brave boy or girl
- Athletic daughter or son
- Popular kid in school
- Boy or girl
- Son or daughter

Ask student volunteers to stand on top of one of the sets of footprints. Then have two students act out a little scene between the two characters at the same time. After each scene, have a discussion about the importance of seeing things from other people's shoes and the concept of empathy.

Here are some suggested scenes that can be acted out:

1. A brave boy or girl is walking among his or her friends when they see a smaller boy. His or her friends make fun of the smaller boy. What should he or she say and do?
2. An athletic daughter or son is walking with his or her tired father, and they come to a set of stairs. What should he or she do?
3. There's a new person who has come to your school, and he or she has no friends. What should the popular kid do?
4. A boy or girl is walking home, and he or she sees an older woman having trouble carrying her groceries. What should he or she do?
5. A son or daughter sees that his or her mother or father is working very long hours and is very tired from work. What can he or she do?

Think of other people in other scenarios and have the students act them out.

ACTIVITY ONE: RIGHT AND WRONG

Answer the following questions in the spaces provided below.

Adnaan is hungry, so he is stealing from the market. Is this right or wrong?
_____

Why?
_____
_____

Karthik wants to call the police. Is this right or wrong?
_____

Why?
_____
_____

Bharat thinks they should give him a second chance. Is this wrong or right?
_____

Why?
_____
_____

TAKE-HOME ACTIVITY

NAME: _____

ARMAN THE CHEAT

Story Summary

When Shahzaman gets caught cheating at backgammon, Shahrzad tells him the story of another boy who also liked to cheat. Things didn't turn out so well for him:

A young boy named Arman forgets to do his homework, so he copies his friend Jasper's paper without Jasper realizing it. When they get their graded papers back from the teacher, Arman receives a perfect score. Since the papers are exactly the same, however, the teacher accuses Jasper of copying Arman's homework. Arman's sister figures out what happened and tells Jasper. Arman is forced to confess, but when he tells the teacher the truth, the teacher thinks he's covering for Jasper. Arman gets away with cheating! The only problem is that the teacher now selects Arman to represent the class in the district-wide math competition, because his grade was so good on his homework. In order to continue the lie, Arman sneaks into the school late at night and steals the answers for the competition to cheat once again. He scores first place in the competition, but when the teacher finds he has the answers to the test in his pocket, Arman's lies catch up with him, and he learns that cheaters may prosper at first, but in the end, they will always get caught.

Story Lessons
- Help children understand that cheating is wrong.
- Show children that if a student cheats in school instead of working hard, he or she will never master skills that may be needed later.
- Help children realize that cheaters eventually get caught.

CLASS PLAN

Pre-Viewing Activity (Approximately 5 Minutes)

Imagine you are playing your favorite game with a friend, such as chess or backgammon, and you discover that your friend is cheating. How does this make you feel? Write down a list of words to describe your reaction to your friend cheating. Possible words might include: angry, betrayed, sad, or frustrated.

Brainstorm some answers. Why do people cheat? In general, cheaters are trying to get some reward (such as a high grade on a test) or to avoid an unwanted outcome (such as losing a sports game). People cheat because they are too lazy to get what they want through hard work. They also might think that they will get away with cheating. What are the consequences of cheating and why is it wrong?

Watch or Read Episode (Approximately 10 Minutes)

Post-Viewing Discussion Questions (Approximately 10 Minutes)

Before this story, Arman was an excellent student and earned good grades. Why do you think he started cheating?
(*Discussion:* Arman was lazy and wanted to play games rather than put in the hard work of studying and doing his homework.)

There's an old saying that goes "Lying has no legs," which means that liars eventually fall down. Do you agree with this saying? Why or why not?
(*Discussion:* People who cheat can't really run away from being caught. Any victories they win are hollow because they were gotten through deceit. People who are winners would prefer to fail or do poorly than to win by cheating.)

If a friend asked to copy your answers during a test, what would you do? Why?
(*Discussion:* Student responses will vary. Make sure to emphasize that letting a classmate copy answers is wrong, and it could get both of you into trouble. It also prevents your friend from learning and showing the teacher what he or she really does or doesn't know.)

In-Class Activity – for 50-60 Minute Lessons (Approximately 30 Minutes)

To help children focus on why cheating is wrong, have them create a campaign for younger students in their school. As a class, or in small groups, have students create posters with slogans, write songs, and perform short skits in which a person cheats (and is caught). Each project could help students explore the reasons why people cheat, and give them reasons for why cheating is harmful. Cheating in school can lead to punishment, or even expulsion, but it also prevents the cheating student from learning skills and information that could help them later on. In addition, students who are caught cheating lose respect from their peers and teachers. Each campaign should also talk about the benefits of working hard and being honest (learning new information and skills, feeling proud about a personal accomplishment, earning the respect of the class, parents, and teachers, etc.).

ACTIVITY ONE: CAUGHT IN THE ACT

Shahzaman sees a jar of candy and wants some. He doesn't see anyone around, so he thinks he can get away with just taking a couple of pieces.

Do you think he will get caught? Why or why not?

_____

_____

_____

If Shahzaman is caught, what do you think will happen?

_____

_____

_____

If Shahzaman is NOT caught, what do you think will happen?

_____

_____

_____

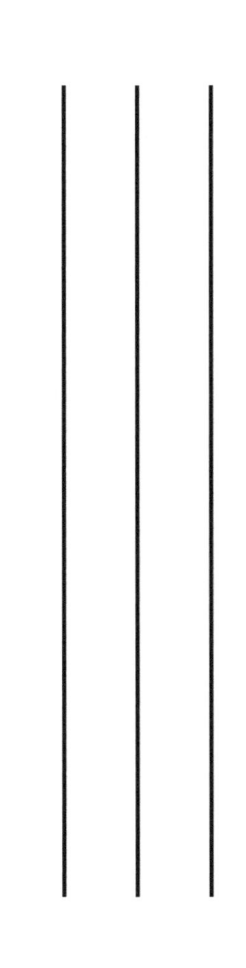
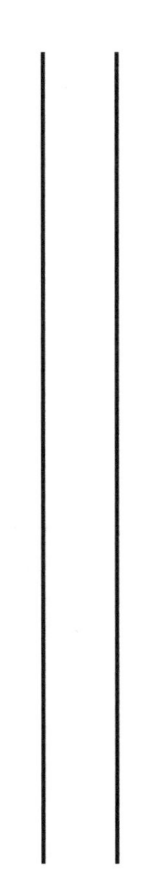

If Shahazaman asked you for advice, what would you tell him?

_____

_____

_____

TAKE-HOME ACTIVITY

NAME: _____

ACTIVITY TWO: HONEST MISTAKES

Interview a family member or friend about a time when he or she was *tempted* to cheat, but ultimately didn't. Use this page to help you record the information from the interview.

Name of person interviewed: _____

Date of interview: _____

What was the person tempted to do? _____

_____

How did the person make the difficult decision to take the honest route? _____

_____

What advice does the family member have for the student if they are ever in a situation in which cheating might seem the right thing to do? _____

_____

TAKE-HOME ACTIVITY

_____

NAME: _____

THE KING WHO BECAME A SLAVE

Story Summary

When Shahzaman doesn't know that one of his servants is having a birthday, Shahrzad tells him it's a leader's responsibility to know what's going on in the lives of the people who work for him. She tells him this story:

King Malik is a spoiled monarch who cares only for himself. When he is accidentally thrown from his carriage, he tumbles down an embankment and lands in a rock quarry where slaves toil. With his clothes torn and ragged from the fall, Malik appears to be one of the slaves. Malik insists he is the king, but the guards don't believe him, so he is imprisoned and forced to work with the other slaves. He endures hardship and learns what life is like as a slave. Appalled at the conditions in prison, Malik unintentionally leads a revolt against the king (himself!), and the slaves now want to overthrow the king! When it is finally revealed to them that Malik is the king, they feel shocked and betrayed. He apologizes for not knowing what was going on in his own kingdom, and he frees them all. He learns that, as king, it is his duty to keep himself informed on everything that goes on in his kingdom.

Story Lessons
- Encourage children to treat others the way they want to be treated. By learning about the struggles and unhappiness of others, we can try to figure out ways to improve their situation through small acts of kindness.
- Help children learn that political leaders have a responsibility to know the needs and wants of all the people they represent, and to help protect them from hardship.

CLASS PLAN

Pre-Viewing Activity (Approximately 5 Minutes)

To help students imagine themselves in another person's shoes (aka empathy), tell them to imagine they are the owner of a restaurant. Show them contrasting photographs taken from the Internet or magazines, of three people (who are not famous), all men: (a muscular athlete, a well-groomed man in a business suit, and an elderly man who appears very poor). Ask them to imagine that each of these people came into your restaurant as a potential customer. How would you treat them if, at the end of the meal, they say, "I'm so sorry, I forgot my money at home. Can I bring it to you later?" How do you (as the restaurant owner) feel about each of the potential customers? Discuss how people's appearances can influence how we respond to them.

Watch or Read Episode (Approximately 10 Minutes)

Post-Viewing Discussion Questions (Approximately 10 Minutes)

Why does King Malik treat his slaves with such little respect at the start of the story?
(*Discussion:* King Malik believes that slaves are not as important as kings.)

Why is it the responsibility of a leader (king, prime minister, president) to know about his or her people?
(*Discussion:* A leader cannot truly lead a group of people if he or she doesn't know what his or her people need in order to be happy and productive. If a leader ignores the needs and burdens of his or her people, then he or she is likely to run into trouble.)

What would it feel like to have someone jump to the wrong conclusion about you?
(*Discussion:* Student responses will vary. Hopefully, students might share stories of times when someone made judgments about them based on superficial details. When we take time to really get to know others, we learn that people are more complex than we might think.)

How does King Malik treat people at the end of the story? Why is his attitude different? Why is this important?
(*Discussion:* After meeting the slaves, experiencing their lives, and knowing their plight, Malik felt bad, and he realized that the slaves were being treated very unfairly. He also realized that he should not have judged them because they were slaves, but should have understood them as people. It is important not to judge people, but rather to try to see things from their perspective.)

In-Class Activity – for 50-60 Minute Lessons (Approximately 30 Minutes)

Ask students how they feel when someone celebrates their birthday. Talk about how students can share that good feeling by making a point of celebrating others' birthdays as well. One way to show interest in another person is to learn when his or her birthday is and, at the very least, say, "Happy birthday." Students are often aware of the birthdays of their peers, but rarely think about the birthdays of grown-ups. The In-Class Activity would be for students to do some detective work and find out the birthdays of teachers, custodians, and other support staff in the school (the calendar date, the year the person was born is not necessary!). The class would make a big list of the birthdays, and then figure out a plan to create a card from the class to each person. These cards would not need to be elaborate, but would at least say "Happy birthday" and be signed by all students, perhaps with pictures.

ACTIVITY ONE: SMALL ACTS OF KINDNESS

Sometimes little actions, such as holding the door for stranger, or saying thank you to a teacher, can make a BIG difference in that person's day.

As your goal this week, do as many little acts of kindness as you can. Don't worry about getting credit for them—take pleasure from knowing that you're making the world a better place.

Here are some ideas to get you started:

* Smile! Say hello to three people you don't know.

* Clean up your room without being asked.

* Compliment someone on his or her clothes.

* Pick up litter at a local park.

* Say I'm sorry when you've done something wrong.

* Start a conversation with an elderly person.

* Hide spare change where someone will find it in a few minutes.

If you have any other ideas for acts of kindness, you can add them here:

_____

_____

_____

NAME: _____

TAKE-HOME ACTIVITY

Imagine that someone suddenly granted you enormous control over every country in the world.
What would you do if you ruled the world for ONE DAY?

Write down five decisions you would make to help others? How would each of these decisions help other people?

1. _____

_____

2. _____

_____

3. _____

_____

4. _____

_____

5. _____

_____

You don't need to be a king to help other people. Can you think of some smaller actions that you can do today to help others? For example, in the first question, you might have written, "I would banish hunger!" but in the real-world version, you might say, "I would give food to someone who is hungry."

_____

_____

_____

TAKE-HOME ACTIVITY

NAME: _____

THE SPOON THAT RUINED EVERYTHING

Note: Teachers will need to have metal spoons for the Pre-Viewing Activity.

Story Summary

Donyazad and Shahzaman are fighting over a seashell – each thinks it is theirs and used for a different purpose - Shahrzad stops their argument by telling them they are both wrong. The shell is a hairpin and it belongs to Shahrzad. She then tells them the story of a tribe of people who turned against one another over a spoon. She tells them this tale:

In a remote part of ancient Mongolia, two explorers, who are passing through, accidentally drop a metal spoon in the grass. A local native named Bataar finds it, and he is astonished to find that it reflects a beam of light. He brings the spoon home and shows it to his tribe. The entire village gathers and delights in watching the sunbeam dance around. His friend Sukh tries it, but just as he takes the spoon, a cloud covers the sun, so the sunbeam disappears. Bataar believes Sukh has broken the spoon. Angry, he takes it back. Inside his hut, he accidentally drops the spoon, and he is surprised when it makes a ringing sound. Delighted, he shows it to the tribe and makes music with it. Sukh carves a spoon out of wood, but he is confused when it won't make the same sound. He offers to trade, but Bataar refuses. They fight over the spoon, and it gets bent. Believing it's ruined, Bataar hurls the spoon to the ground, and it bounces around like a spring. It lands in the mouth of an attacking panther and chokes him to death. The tribe now believes the spoon is magical, and they fight over it. Friendships disintegrate and the group is fractured by greed. In the end, they learn that their friendship is more important than even a "magic" spoon.

Story Lessons
- Encourage children to appreciate their relationships with others, and to realize that material goods are not more valuable than friendship and family.
- Inspire children to share their possessions with others. Help them realize that there are many ways to share any object, if one is creative and flexible. Sharing can bring great happiness.

CLASS PLAN

Pre-Viewing Activity (Approximately 5 Minutes)

Divide students into groups. Give each group a metal spoon and challenge them to write a list of as many things as they can that a spoon might be used for. Encourage them to be creative and think of usual and unusual things. Students might come up with a list that includes eating soup; firing a small object like a catapult; making music; stirring together ingredients; using the back as a mirror; something shiny to entertain a baby; and so on.

Ask students if they think they could get into a fight with a friend over a large amount of money they both found in the street. Then ask if they could fight about a small amount of money they found, and finally, a tiny amount of money, such as a single coin. Point out that fighting over money, no matter the amount, is not something friends should do. What about fighting over something as silly as a spoon? After listening to all responses, share this episode, and ask students to look for the reasons behind why the characters fight with one another.

Watch or Read Episode (Approximately 10 Minutes)

Post-Viewing Discussion Questions (Approximately 10 Minutes)

Why do you think Bataar and Sukh fought so much over a spoon? Can you think of some ways they could have shared it?
(*Discussion:* These men argued over the spoon because there was only one, and they were more concerned with owning it than with thinking about their friendship. Rather than arguing about it, they could have taken turns using the spoon and appreciated each other's discoveries rather than worrying about who gets credit for finding out the spoon's different uses.)

If Bataar and Sukh had figured out ways to share the spoon, how do you think things would have turned out differently?
(*Discussion:* Had the two men found ways to share the spoon, then they would have celebrated their discovery rather than making it a reason for arguing.)

What do you think might have happened if, in the middle of the story, someone had found a big box of spoons, so that there was enough for everyone in the town to have one?
(*Discussion:* If they shared the spoons, many of the people would have fought less over the spoons because there would have been enough for everyone. But, if they all behaved in a greedy way, then they would have found a way to argue over who should get the most spoons, which spoons were the best, and so on.)

In-Class Activity – for 50-60 Minute Lessons (Approximately 30 Minutes)

To reinforce the theme of fighting over limited resources, ask students to think of times that they have argued with a sibling or friend over an object that they found, such as an old toy, a coin, or an interesting rock or stick. How did it make them feel to argue over something like this? Was the item worth the argument or its consequences?

To strengthen relationships among classmates, students can play this game. Have each student write his or her name on a piece of paper, followed by a number from 1 to 10 (important that students don't see what others are writing). Then, ask all the students with "1" next to their name to come to one section of the classroom, all students with "2" next to their name to another section of the classroom, and so on. All the students in each group then write down five things they have in common with the others in their group, such as the color of their clothes, their favorite snack, their favorite sport, etc. Near the end of class, all the groups discuss what it felt like to have something in common with another person.

ACTIVITY ONE: WHEN SHARING ISN'T EASY

What would you do if...

Imagine on your birthday, you get a gift that you know your friend has wanted for a long time. You are excited to play with it and your friend asks if he or she can borrow it. What would you do?

_____

_____

_____

_____

What would you do if your friend discovered they forgot to take their lunch to school with them?

_____

_____

_____

TAKE-HOME ACTIVITY

NAME: _____

In this *1,001 Nights* story, the characters fight over an object and forget what is truly important and valuable: friendships.

First, think of a friend who is very important to you.

Write down five reasons why you think this friend is so important:

1. _____
2. _____
3. _____
4. _____
5. _____

Is your friend more important to you than your toys? _____

Why? _____

_____

_____

What are some activities that you can do with friends that you can't do with objects (such as toys)? For example, you can talk with your friend, make jokes, and so on.

_____

_____

_____

Keep this list handy. Next time you feel an argument coming, look at the list and remember all of the things that make your friends so special.

THE KING WHO OUTLAWED LAUGHTER

Story Summary

When Shahzaman slips and falls off the diving board, Donyazad laughs and makes fun of him. Shahzaman gets mad, but Shahrzad tells him it's okay to laugh at himself. She says there once was a king who was so sensitive to others' comments that he made life miserable for everyone around him. She tells him this story:

On the day of his coronation, King Raheem slips and falls into a cake. Everyone laughs at him, and he is so humiliated that he outlaws laughter in his kingdom forever more. Life is miserable in the kingdom, and nobody smiled until, one day, a traveling troupe of performers is passing through town. They do a comedy act that has everyone laughing, which gets the performers arrested. King Raheem sentences one of them to die, but he allows them to choose which one of them will drown in the moat. They send their magician, because he's also an escape artist. After being thrown into the moat, he slips out of the chains and swims back to the surface. The town is in awe and cheers, but the king is furious, and he orders another of them to die -this person to be burned at the stake. The troupe sends their fire-eater, who quickly extinguishes the flames. Again the town cheers, and Raheem, furious, now orders his guards to throw one of the performers off the castle walls. They choose the acrobat who swings from one flagpole to another and lands safely on the ground. So Raheem orders them all to be fed to the tigers. One of the performers is an animal trainer. He calms the tigers and has them doing tricks. Raheem gives up and orders the performers to leave the kingdom and never come back. When the performers stumble over one another trying to get out the door and break into a pie fight, King Raheem laughs, and soon the entire court is howling. The king learns to smile again, and laughter returns to the kingdom once more.

Story Lessons
- Help children learn the value of not taking themselves too seriously, and seeing the benefits of laughing at their own mistakes.
- Help children understand that people in a position of power should act responsibly.
- Help children understand that laughter is a wonderful thing, but it can sometimes be hurtful. There's a difference between playfully "laughing with" and cruelly "laughing at" someone.

CLASS PLAN

Pre-Viewing Activity (Approximately 5 Minutes)

Ask students to raise their hands if they think they have a good sense of humor. Then ask: What do we mean when we say that someone has a "good sense of humor"? Does it mean that the person laughs a lot? Does it mean that the person makes others laugh a lot? What does it mean to say that people have a good sense of humor about themselves? Help students understand that part of having a good sense of humor is a willingness to laugh at one's own mistakes, and not take oneself too seriously.

What's the difference between laughing at someone vs. laughing at oneself? In the discussion, point out that the former action can be mean, and hurt someone's feelings, whereas the latter can bring people closer together.

Watch or Read Episode (Approximately 10 Minutes)

Post-Viewing Discussion Questions (Approximately 10 Minutes)

Why do you think King Raheem has such a hard time with people laughing at him?
(*Discussion:* He believes people are making fun of him, not the situation. When people laugh, it often isn't meant to be mean or harmful, but rather because the situation strikes them as funny (like a funny hat, or when we spill something). The king takes himself much too seriously. He doesn't realize that learning to laugh at oneself is a good quality, especially in a leader, because it makes him more likeable and approachable. When he outlawed laughter, he sent a harmful message to his people.)

When the king outlawed laughter, do you think he was acting appropriately?
(*Discussion:* No, the king outlawing laughter was an overreaction to his feeling embarrassed about falling. Since the king took himself too seriously, he abused his power and made a very strict law that was also impossible to enforce. The law also made his people lose respect for him.)

Imagine that you are carrying an armful of eggs, when you get a fit of hiccups and you accidentally trip, dropping the eggs. All but one of them fall and crack, and several splatter on your head. You're not hurt, but it's a mess. Fortunately, there is no one else around. How do you react? Will you tell others later about your egg-venture?
(*Discussion:* It depends. If you are unable to see the humor in the situation, you might become frustrated and angry at first. If you can find the humor, however, you might chuckle to yourself, wipe off the egg, clean the floor, maybe cook the one remaining egg for lunch, then go about your day. Later, you might tell a friend about what happened, so they can appreciate the humor too.)

Imagine that another student is running and falls in the playground. What are some ways you could respond?
(*Discussion:* First, you would want to go over to the student to see if he or she is injured. Then, knowing that this type of situation can be embarrassing, you might let the person know that it's okay, everyone has times like this. If you take the opposite approach and laugh at the person for falling, chances are that person's feelings will be hurt, and this person might laugh at you one day if you have an accident.)

In-Class Activity – for 50-60 Minute Lessons (Approximately 30 Minutes)

To help students understand that those in power have a responsibility to act responsibly and appropriately, present them with this fictional situation:

Late one afternoon, a mother asks her 16-year-old son, Samir, to babysit for his younger sister, Aisha, while she visits a sick neighbor. Samir is very proud of himself but is now in a position of responsibility and power. What will he do? Before going, his mother reminds Samir that he needs to make sure Aisha finishes her homework, and that both children clean up their rooms.

Vote on, and discuss, which of the following acts would be appropriate for Samir to ask Aisha to do while his mother is away.

- Samir insists Aisha complete her homework completely before playing games.
- Samir makes Aisha clean up his bedroom so that he can watch TV.
- Samir tells Aisha she has to help clean up the spill she made while eating a snack.
- Samir tells Aisha to sharpen his pencils while he's drawing pictures.
- Samir insists that Aisha clean his shoes, which are very muddy.
- Samir asks Aisha to help him pick up one of the toys that he left on kitchen floor.

Brainstorm with the class to think of other things Samir could ask Aisha to do and decide what is appropriate and what is not. Then discuss why it is important for Samir to make sure he is fair and appropriate.

ACTIVITY ONE: LOOK WHAT I DID

LESSON THIRTY FIVE

Directions: Can you figure out three funny captions for these pictures? Try to show each character saying something that shows he can laugh at him or herself.

Figure 1: _____

Figure 2: _____

Figure 3: _____

TAKE-HOME ACTIVITY

NAME: _____

THE MAN WHO WENT BACK IN TIME

Story Summary

Shahzaman is angry when another boy is chosen to be captain of the soccer team. He says the only reason the other boy was picked is because his father is the coach. Shahrzad reminds him that just getting lucky breaks in life isn't enough. One has to work hard and make the most of opportunities. She tells him a story of a man who thought success was all about luck and had little to do with hard work:

Faadi was a man with no ambition. He lived in his mother's garage, where he ran an old pawnshop. Fed up with his laziness, his mother asks why he can't be more like his successful neighbor, Sarim. Faadi tells her that the only reason Sarim is successful is because years ago he got a lucky break. When his mother leaves, Faadi opens a box, and a genie named Gajinder appears. Gajinder tells Faadi he is granted one wish; however, Faadi is allowed to keep re-wishing until he's satisfied. Faadi wishes for Gajinder to take him back in time so that he can get Sarim's lucky break. When he returns to the present, however, nothing has changed. The lucky break didn't change things for him because he failed to take advantage of the opportunity and work hard. In the meantime, Sarim has gone on to be successful at something else. Faadi now wishes to follow Sarim's new path, but once again, he winds up a failure. No matter what he does, Faadi fails because he has no work ethic. Conversely, because he's honest and works hard, Sarim succeeds, regardless of what path he takes. Shahzaman learns that success is primarily a result of hard work, not luck. It's not the breaks you get in life, but what you do with them.

Story Lessons
- Help children understand that success comes from hard work, commitment, and honesty. There are no short cuts in life.
- Everyone, no matter their background or connections, can succeed if they make the most of opportunities, are willing to work hard, and persist toward their goals.

CLASS PLAN

Pre-Viewing Activity (Approximately 5 Minutes)

Ask students to think about which is more important in order to achieve success: good luck or hard work. The answer is actually both. In the discussion, point out that while luck certainly plays a role (such as a musically talented child being born in a town that has a top-notch music school), it is something we cannot control. Hard work, on the other hand, is something that we can definitely affect. Ask students to think of two runners who are preparing for a race. One of the runners is bigger and stronger than the other, but he takes these natural gifts for granted. He eats poorly and does not train at all. The other runner, who is naturally smaller and weaker, eats healthy food and trains every day. If these two people were to race against each other, who do you think would win?

As students watch the episode/read the story, have them look for examples of how the character of Sarim uses hard work to achieve success in a variety of jobs.

Watch or Read Episode (Approximately 10 Minutes)

Post-Viewing Discussion Questions (Approximately 10 Minutes)

Why do you think Faadi believes that he could easily have all of Sarim's wealth and success?
(*Discussion:* Faadi thinks that success is purely a result of luck, being in the right place at the right time. By only paying attention to Sarim's lucky breaks and final achievements, he overlooks all the important steps, and hard work, that made Sarim successful. Faadi would only have become as successful as Sarim if he had followed Sarim's work ethic and put in the necessary effort.)

When Faadi is an unsuccessful musician, the genie tells him, "Talent without hard work is nothing." Do you agree? Why or why not?
(*Discussion:* The genie wants Faadi to understand that we all have natural talents, but if we don't work hard, our talents will remain underdeveloped. Faadi has a powerful patron in the genie, who creates opportunities for him, but Faadi doesn't make the most of them.)

Every time Faadi picks a profession, he is unsuccessful and Sarim is successful. Why? Is Sarim just lucky and Faadi unlucky?
(*Discussion:* Sarim is successful because he works hard. Faadi is unsuccessful because he doesn't work hard. Faadi could have been just as successful as Sarim if he worked hard, was honest and was diligent.)

What do you think is the moral of this story?
(*Discussion:* Success is due to many things, some of which are out of our control. We should focus on those things, such as hard work, which we can control. Everyone, no matter their background or connections, can succeed if they make the most of opportunities, are willing to work hard, and persist toward their goals.)

In-Class Activity – for 50-60 Minute Lessons (Approximately 30 Minutes)

To help students explore how success comes from honest, hard work versus fast, good luck, have them consider key moments from a fictional person's life. The person's name is Hamid. If Hamid wants to succeed in life, what can he do in each of the following situations to make himself successful?

Hamid is born into a poor family, who loves and cares for him. His teachers tell him he's bright and talented. They say he has the potential to go far if he does well in school. There is also a library near his house. The library holds a reading and writing competition for students. The top prize is a year's worth of school supplies and books—for free. What can Hamid do to help his chances of winning this competition?

At age nine, Hamid is invited to try out for the local soccer team. He loves to play soccer but hasn't played in a while. What could he do before the tryouts to boost his chances of making the team?

In high school, Hamid hears about a competition in which students in his area can go on a local TV program to try to answer questions about math, science, and literature. The winner of this competition wins a scholarship to college! What can he do to prepare for this contest?

As an adult, Hamid wants to open a restaurant. He enjoys cooking, and he took business in school. What can he do before he opens the restaurant to increase his chances of people really liking the food and making it a big success?

If Hamid works hard and is successful, is he successful because he is lucky or for another reason? Discuss.

ACTIVITY ONE: WHAT WOULD SARIM DO?

Directions: In the story, "The man who went back in time", Sarim, is successful because he does things differently than Faadi. He makes the most of every opportunity. Look at the pictures and words below and use your knowledge of Sarim to write what actions he might take.

Sarim is getting ready to visit a nearby city to look for a job. He heard that many businesses in the area are looking to hire people. What would Sarim do to prepare for this trip?

_____

_____

_____

_____

Sarim's neighbor asks Sarim if he would like to borrow some of his land to plant a small vegetable garden. The neighbor says that a successful garden takes plenty of care. Sarim is interested but has never planted a garden before. What would Sarim do?

_____

_____

_____

Sarim just learned that the town is holding a race to raise money for a local charity. The winner will also get his or her picture in the paper. What would Sarim do?

_____

_____

_____

TAKE-HOME ACTIVITY

NAME: _____

PRINCESS ROU

Note: Prior to class, teachers will need to make multiple copies of Activity Sheet One.

Story Summary

When Shahzaman easily defeats Donyazad at arm wrestling, she becomes discouraged and believes that she's weaker than Shahzaman. Shahrzad explains to her that she too can be strong. She tells her the story of Princess Rou:

Emperor Ghouzi is getting old and wants his daughter, Princess Rou, to get married, so there will be a male heir to the throne. The only problem: his strong, athletic and fiercely independent daughter Rou, has no desire to wed. As a compromise, she tells her father she will marry a prince if he can find one who can defeat her in physical combat. Her father arranges to have her battle with the three greatest warriors in the kingdom, confident that at least one of them will best her. When she defeats them all, the king furiously orders her to get married. Rou's meek and loyal servant, Xiaodan, yells at the king, telling him that Rou is perfectly capable of ruling the kingdom as well as any man. As he speaks, Rou realizes that Xiaodan is in love with her and that she loves him. Just as the king is about to punish Xiaodan for his outburst, Rou demands that Xiaodan battle her in the ring. When they fight, Rou lets Xiaodan win, making him the victor of her hand in marriage. The two are married, and Rou goes on to rule the kingdom with Xiaodan happily at her side.

Story Lessons
- Increase children's awareness of gender stereotypes and help them realize how such stereotypes can limit personal growth, and even harm society.
- Encourage children to develop a wide range of interests, without worrying about whether the interests are more popular with boys or girls.

CLASS PLAN

Pre-Viewing Activity (Approximately 5 Minutes)

Before class, write ten out of the following descriptive sentences on the board:

- Super strong
- Shy
- Loves to cook
- Enjoys playing sports
- Is a doctor
- Is a great leader
- Will one day be prime minister
- Enjoys singing
- Works late at the office
- Enjoys gardening
- Is very funny
- Stays home and takes care of the children
- Earns a lot of money

Tell the students that there are several characteristics written on the board, and they should be assigned to two people and all they know are their names: Zahra and Amir. Read aloud the list of attributes and ask each student to think about which of the two people fits each attribute, but not to say their opinions out loud (for the purpose of this activity, each attribute can only be assigned either to Zahra or Amir, not both). After two minutes, read each attribute aloud and ask how many people said Amir was super strong? How many said that Zahra was the super strong one? Based on the majority, somehow connect the "super strong" label to either Amir or Zahra (you could write Amir and Zahra on the board, then under each person's name, write the attributes that the students select by vote). Go through each attribute in this manner and have a general discussion about the results and why people feel this way.

Explain the word "stereotype" – a stereotype is when society holds beliefs about what a person is or should be because of a certain characteristic (like boys are strong, girls are weak, or people from a certain region are untrustworthy). Ask students to look for stereotypes in the story they are about to see (or hear) — and people who defy those stereotypes.

Watch or Read Episode (Approximately 10 Minutes)

Post-Viewing Discussion Questions (Approximately 10 Minutes)

What stereotypes about men and women did you see in the story?
(*Discussion*: Emperor Ghouzi's three warriors are all physically strong males so they are seen to be ideal suitors for Princess Rou. Xiaodan, who is meek and a servant is not considered a viable mate for Princess Rou. Also, one warrior jokes that the groom is prettier than the bride. In this case, the stereotype is that women are not supposed to be strong, they are supposed to be pretty and meek.)

How do you think people learn stereotypes?
(*Discussion*: People learn stereotypes from their family, their community, as well as images they see in magazines, movies and on television).

Why did Emperor Ghouzi want his daughter to get married? Does that sound like a good reason to you? Why? Why not?

(*Discussion:* Emperor Ghouzi believes that his daughter needs to get married, so that her husband can rule the kingdom when he dies. He doesn't realize that Princess Rou would make an excellent leader because he assumes only boys can be leaders.)

In-Class Activity – for 50-60 Minute Lessons (Approximately 30 Minutes)

To help students personalize the educational objectives, help them think about what activities they enjoy, regardless of whether they are stereotypically done by boys or girls.

Hand each child an illustrated list of activities (Activity Sheet One handout). Ask students to circle the things they like to do. This should be done secretly, so that each child feels free to honestly list his or her own interests. Circle "boy" or "girl" at the top of the page to indicate their gender, but do not ask them to put their name on the page. Collect all the lists and then tally the votes for each activity (providing the number of boys and girls that liked to do each activity).

Lead a discussion about why the boys and girls picked each one and why it would be acceptable for both to like the activity.

LESSON THIRTY SEVEN

ACTIVITY ONE: CHOOSE WHAT'S RIGHT FOR YOU!

Are you a boy or a girl? Circle one. BOY   GIRL

Directions: Circle any of the activities that you enjoy doing. Don't worry about what choices other children might make. This is a secret ballot. The important thing is that you are honest about what *you* like to do.

IN-CLASS ACTIVITY

NAME: _____

ACTIVITY TWO: HELP THE CO-RULERS

At the end of the story, Princess Rou and Xiaodan decide to rule their empire together. They firmly believe that anyone can do whatever activities they enjoy. What can they do to encourage people not to have stereotypes? How do you think they raised their children? Write a short story and draw a picture that tells about a day in the lives of this family.

TAKE-HOME ACTIVITY

NAME: _____

TWO KIDS AND A GENIE

Story Summary

A shop owner named Gamal has two assistants, a boy named Nasim and a girl named Badra. Nasim causes damage in the shop, but blames Badra for it in front of Gamal. Frustrated with Badra, Gamal puts Nasim in charge of the shop while he goes out to run errands. He locks a strange-looking bottle in a drawer and tells them not to touch it. As soon as he leaves, Nasim breaks the lock with a screwdriver and takes out the bottle. Against Badra's protests, Nasim opens the bottle and a genie comes out. The genie proceeds to wreak havoc, bringing things to life that destroy the shop. When he brings a dragon statue to life, the dragon breathes fire and crushes everything in his path. As the dragon is about to eat the kids, he is sucked into a pair of bellows by Gamal, who returns just in time. He also traps the genie and places him back inside the bottle. Nasim once again blames Badra, telling Gamal that she's the one who let the genie out of the bottle. Outraged, Badra reaches into Nasim's shirt pocket and pulls out the stopper to the bottle. When Gamal sees it, he knows Nasim is lying. Nasim is forced to clean the shop by himself, while Gamal and Badra sip tea from behind the counter.

Story Lessons
- Help children realize that making someone else look bad doesn't make you look better, and it will eventually catch up to you.
- Help children realize that, while it is important to try to improve oneself, it is wrong to use methods that hurt other people.
- Encourage students to treat one another's property with respect.

CLASS PLAN

Pre-Viewing Activity (Approximately 5 Minutes)

Tell students something like: Imagine that the principal came into the classroom to tell me that I had an important phone call, and I had to leave the classroom for ten minutes. What do you think might happen while I was away? What would you do if anyone started to misbehave? Whether children say they would behave or misbehave, use their answers as a springboard to discuss acting responsibly.

Watch or Read Episode (Approximately 3 Minutes)

Note that this episode is only three minutes long and has no dialogue.

Post-Viewing Discussion Questions (Approximately 10 Minutes)

Even though the shop owner told the kids that the bottle was off-limits, Nasim broke into the drawer and removed the bottle. Why do you think Nasim didn't listen to the owner's wishes?
(*Discussion:* Nasim didn't listen to the owner because he put his own wishes before others. He selfishly wanted to satisfy his curiosity rather than listen to the owner, who knew that opening the bottle would lead to trouble.)

Nasim liked it when his boss praised him and gave him more responsibility. The problem was he achieved this success through lying and cheating. Can you think of a different way Nasim could have acted to get more responsibility?
(*Discussion:* Nasim's successes weren't earned fairly. He lied about what happened, and he only looked good because he made Badra look bad. He did not treat either Badra or Gamal with respect. A better way to earn success would be to work hard, treat other people with respect, and work together with Badra so that both of them could succeed.)

When the truth comes out at the end, that Nasim is actually responsible for letting the genie out of the bottle, do you think it is right that Nasim is forced to clean the shop by himself? Why or why not?
(*Discussion:* Student responses will vary. Nasim was the one who caused much of the trouble in the shop, so he is the one who should clean it up. He was punished for lying, trying to make someone else look bad, and for disrespecting someone else's property.)

How would you feel if you and another friend were helping out a neighbor clean up their house, and the friend started making it look like he or she did all the work and you were making a mess of things, when in reality, you both worked together? How do you think you could help the situation?
(*Discussion:* Having a friend make you look bad, or him- or herself look good at your expense, would be upsetting for a number of reasons. It would mean that you might get in trouble for something you didn't do, and it would make you less likely to trust your friend again.)

In-Class Activity – for 50-60 Minute Lessons (Approximately 30 Minutes)

To help students explore the theme of respecting others' property, ask them to envision these situations and how they might respond.

Imagine that it is lunchtime. Students have already eaten their lunch, but are still a little hungry. A friend at a nearby table asks you to watch the rest of their lunch while he or she goes to the restroom. You notice several pieces of baklava on his or her plate. Is it okay to take just one? Why or why not?

Have a discussion about the concept of personal property and what it means to be responsible and have others trust you. Point out the importance of treating other people's property in the same way you'd like your property to be treated.

Imagine that you forgot your pen. One of your friend's pens falls from his bag while walking, and you know he has several more in his bag. Would you take the pen that fell? Why or why not?

You are in a candy shop. You fill a bag with candies. While waiting in line at the counter, you open one of the candies and eat it. When it is your turn to pay, you realize that you don't have enough money to pay for the bag. What do you do? Do you mention the candy you ate? Do you pay for it? Why or why not?

After you've discussed these scenarios, invite students to suggest their own situations in which they might be tempted to take someone else's personal property.

ACTIVITY ONE: JUST DESSERTS

In the story you saw/heard, Nasim tried to get Badra in trouble. He learned his lesson! Once he was caught, he had to clean up the store while Badra got to relax.

Finish the story below:

One day, a baker in their neighborhood invited Badra and Nasim to help make a special dessert. Both kids are excited, but now Badra is in a mischievous mood. She wants to give Nasim a taste of his own medicine. So when Nasim isn't looking, Badra adds a few ingredients that will make Nasim's food taste bad.

In the space below, write a story about what happens. Does Badra get caught? How?

TAKE-HOME ACTIVITY

NAME: _____

ACTIVITY TWO: EVERYONE WINS!

It is sometimes easy to think that the only way to achieve your goals is to push others out of the way. The truth is that when people work together and respect one another's goals and dreams, more can be accomplished and in a more pleasant way.

Have a family meeting. Together, pick an ambitious goal that the family could work on in the coming week. Maybe it is cleaning the whole house, or creating a decoration for a common room, or preparing a special dinner they will all enjoy.

What goal did you pick?

Break down the goal into different steps and decide who is responsible for each of the steps. If you are cleaning the house, you might each have a particular chore, such as dusting or sweeping. Or if you decide to make a special dinner, one person could be responsible for the shopping, someone else for chopping the ingredients, and another person for setting the table.

What did you enjoy most about working with one another?

What challenges did you overcome during this project?

TAKE-HOME ACTIVITY

NAME: _____

ABU MOHAMMAD LAZYBONES

Story Summary

When Shahzaman puts on Shahryar's crown and pretends to be king, Donyazad asks if she can try it. Shahzaman tells her that girls can't be kings, they're queens. Shahrzad tells him that sometimes the person you least expect can become something you never thought possible. She relates the story of Abu Mohammad Lazybones:

Abu Mohammad lived on a small farm with his mother near the town of Najaf. One day, she sends him into town to fetch groceries and supplies. When he arrives, the town is holding a mayoral election. Mayor Karim, the town's current mayor, shouts to the crowd that he wants growth and prosperity. When he asks Abu Mohammad what he wants, Mohammad says food. The crowd interprets that to mean he wants to put food on everyone's table. They ask him about jobs and work, and he says that work is "taxing." They take that to mean he is for lower taxes. No matter how Abu Mohammad responds, everyone interprets his simple answers to mean something profound. To Karim's horror, Abu Mohammad is elected mayor. Soon the town is prospering because they hear in his plain words, the truth they really want to believe. The emperor becomes so impressed with Abu Mohammad that he makes him his vizier. Within minutes of doing this, the emperor dies and because he has no heir, Mohammad, as his vizier, becomes emperor.

Story Lessons

- Help children to think optimistically about their future. What you never thought was possible can sometimes happen: Life is full of unexpected twists. Everyone has the ability and right to become anything they want to be.
- Encourage children not to underestimate the power of honesty and a good heart to inspire people to follow them.
- True leaders are those that represent the interests of the people and empower people to strive for their best.

CLASS PLAN

Pre-Viewing Activity (Approximately 5 Minutes)

Ask students to brainstorm some examples of great leaders of whom they know. What are some qualities that make a good leader? Some suggestions might be that they are caring, listen to their people, encourage teamwork, work hard, are humble, give credit where credit is due, and have a sense of humor.

As they watch the episode/read the story, have them look for ways that Abu Mohammad is a good leader—even though he has no training or experience.

Watch or Read Episode (Approximately 10 Minutes)

Post-Viewing Discussion Questions (Approximately 10 Minutes)

Why do you think Abu Mohammad was so successful as a mayor?
(*Discussion:* Although Abu Mohammad is a simple farmer, he always answers honestly. People listen to Abu Mohammad with great optimism, and they add more meaning to his words than Abu Mohammad ever intended with his literal answers.)

Do you think that when Abu Mohammad was a boy, he thought he would someday grow up to be emperor? Can we always know what opportunities are waiting for us?
(*Discussion:* As a simple farm boy, Abu Mohammad never would have imagined that he'd one day be mayor or emperor. None of us can know what the future holds, so it's important to believe that you can be anything you want to be, stay open to new opportunities, and be ready to take advantage of opportunities with hard work and dedication when they arise.)

Karim wanted desperately to be mayor, while Abu Mohammad never even thought about it. So, why do you think Abu Mohammad was the one who became mayor?
(*Discussion:* Abu Mohammad approached everyone with honesty and a good heart, whereas Karim was more interested in trying to debase Abu Mohammad than doing something positive for the people he was to serve. People tend to respond best to those who approach them with good intentions and an honest desire to help.)

In-Class Activity – for 50-60 Minute Lessons (Approximately 30 Minutes)

What qualities make a great leader? Why, against all odds, did Abu Mohammad succeed as mayor of his town?

Write the words "Great Leader" in the middle of the board or on a piece of paper on the wall. Then have students brainstorm as many specific qualities that a leader should have to do his or her job. Some suggestions include:

- Humility
- Ability to let people solve their own problems
- Set a good example
- Willingness to work hard
- Ability to inspire teamwork
- Have a sense of humor
- Ability to talk clearly to lots of different kinds of people
- Be informed about the problems in the town

LESSON THIRTY NINE

ACTIVITY ONE: WHAT'S MOST IMPORTANT?

When Abu Mohammad arrives in the new town, he tells the townspeople that he just wants food. The others compliment him on having his priorities straight. Priorities are things that are considered more important than others. Knowing your priorities is like having a map—so you get where you want to go, and do not get distracted by less important pursuits.

Directions: By yourself, create a to-do list of everything you need to do this week, in school and at home. You should have at least ten items on your list. Then, see if you can figure out which three items on your list are your top priorities. What choices are the most difficult? What are the consequences of doing (or NOT doing) each item on your list.

My list of things to do:

1. _____
2. _____
3. _____
4. _____
5. _____
6. _____
7. _____
8. _____
9. _____
10. _____

My top three priorities:

1. _____
2. _____
3. _____

TAKE-HOME ACTIVITY

NAME: _____

ACTIVITY TWO: EXPECT THE UNEXPECTED

In this story, Abu Mohammad, a simple farm boy, was elected mayor. He inspired people, helped his town recover from economic problems, and then became emperor. What would you like to do when you grow up and why? In the space below, draw a picture of yourself twenty years in the future. Below the picture, write a sentence or two that says what you are doing and why you want to do it.

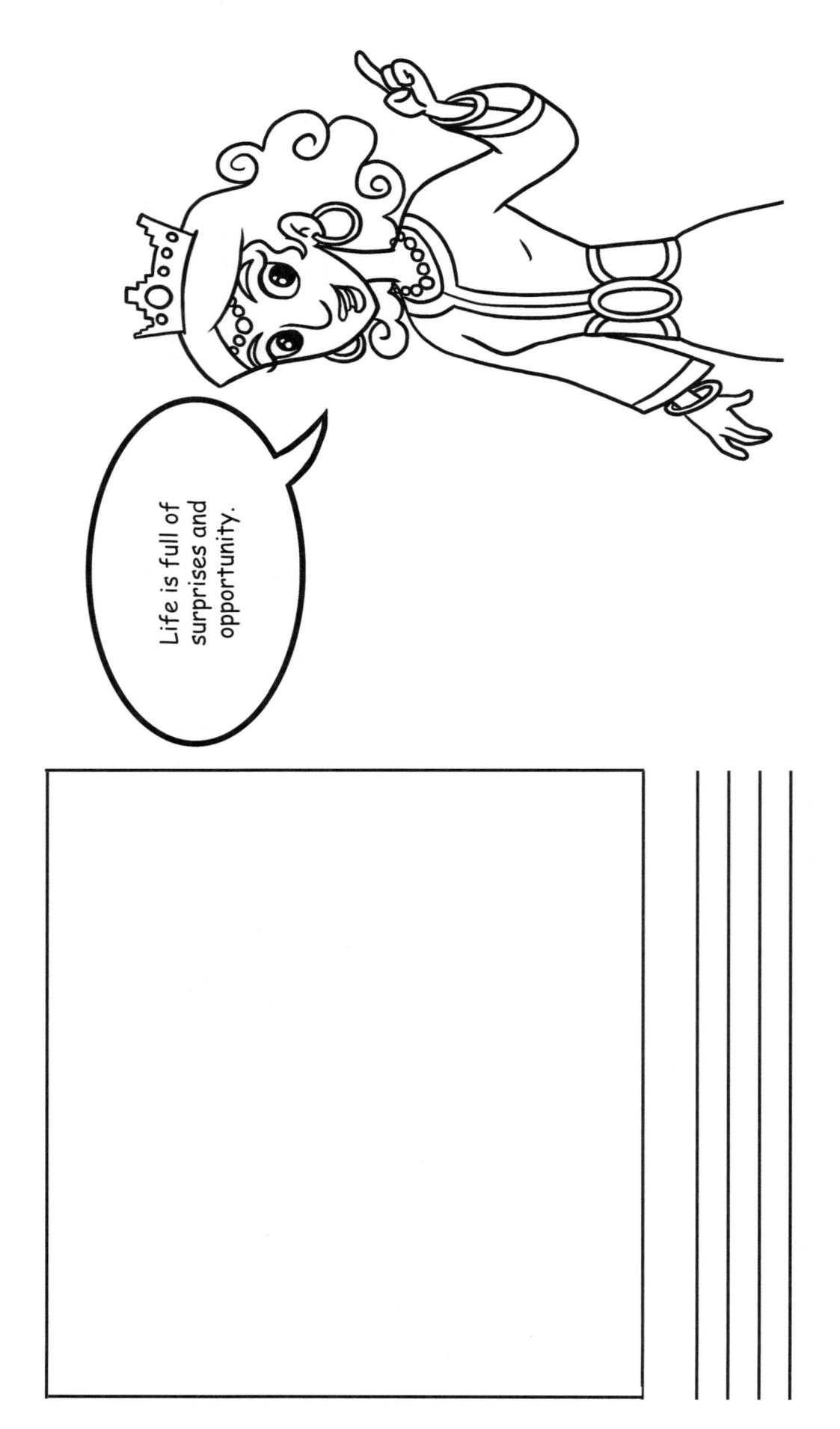

Life is full of surprises and opportunity.

TAKE-HOME ACTIVITY

NAME: _____

ONE THOUSAND AND ONE NIGHTS

Note: As part of the Take-Home Activity sheet, there is a supporting sheet attached to the back of this lesson plan.

Story Summary

The origin of the tales of *One Thousand and One Nights* reveals stories that were handed down from person to person over thousands of years. Beginning with oral tradition, the stories were eventually written down, and then collected from across Asia, the Far East, India, Persia, and Arabia.

A soldier returning from a conquest in China brings back a box he found containing old parchments. He sells those parchments to a shopkeeper, who realizes that they contain stories. She binds them together into a book and sells the book to a traveling merchant. He later stops at an inn and tells a girl there one of the stories in the book. It is the tale that will someday be known as *Cinderella*. Traveling on, he loses the book in a desert sandstorm. A boy and his father find the book, but neither of them can read. The boy doodles on one of the empty pages and inadvertently creates the idea of a genie. He then sells the book to a seafarer, who becomes marooned on an island for twenty years. His story will someday become the tale of *Robinson Crusoe*. The book eventually finds itself in a bookstore, where a young man named Majid purchases it. Majid buys the book for his ten-year-old daughter. The young girl's name is Shahrzad, and she becomes entranced with the stories. She tells her father that someday she might like to tell stories. Of course, she grows up to become one of the world's most famous storytellers.

Story Lessons
- Show children that knowledge is power, and help them understand the importance of reading and studying.
- Help children appreciate the value of stories to entertain and educate people of all ages. Literacy offers many benefts for those who can read and write.
- Inspire children to create their own version of classic stories and folktales.

CLASS PLAN

Pre-Viewing Activity (Approximately 5 Minutes)

Discuss how students in this class have watched or heard many episodes of *1001 Nights*. Ask students if they were familiar with the book *1001 Nights* before this class. Explain that the stories are over 1000 years old and come from all over Asia and North Africa. Many classic stories they know, such as Aladdin, Ali Baba and the Forty Thieves, and Cinderella, have roots in this book. Ask: Why do you think these stories have survived for so long? Briefly discuss what makes a good story.

As they watch/listen to this episode, have students look for ways that everyday events in life give someone an idea for a story or character.

Watch or Read Episode (Approximately 10 Minutes)

Post-Viewing Discussion Questions (Approximately 10 Minutes)

At the end of the story, a young Shahrzad receives an old, tattered book that has traveled around the world. Why do you think it survived, and why did no one throw it out? Do you think this was the only copy of these stories? (*Discussion:* Books are valuable possessions. They carry information and stories that can teach and entertain us in a variety of situations. In this episode, a sailor buys the book of stories from the boy because he wants something to keep him interested while he's at sea. It turned out to be such a good book that everyone who found it discovered something interesting in it. The stories that Shahrzad received were a collection of stories that were written around the world. There were probably many other stories that were in other books.)

Do you think books are good presents? Why or why not? (*Discussion:* Although some people don't think so, books can make excellent presents, as they contain stories and information that the reader can enjoy anytime, anywhere. Books are key to learning new knowledge and passing this knowledge to other generations.)

Would you like to be a storyteller someday? Why or why not? What does it take to be a good storyteller? (*Discussion:* Being a storyteller can be an exciting profession. Storytellers today write books, tell stories in person to school groups, write scripts for TV, movies, comic books, and much more. To be an effective storyteller, one needs to be able to create vivid characters, understand how to plot a story, fill it with surprises, and provide satisfying conclusions.)

What elements make a good story? In other words, what qualities make some stories more engaging than others (and make you eager to know "what happens next?") (*Discussion:* Stories that hold the audience's attention well tend to have characters that the audience cares about and with whom they can relate. Appealing stories also have interesting plots that surprise us. Exciting stories also often have conflict and tension, such as heroes versus villains.)

In-Class Activity – for 50-60 Minute Lessons (Approximately 30 Minutes)

Have students suggest books or movies they especially love and have students analyze why they enjoy them so much. Discuss the elements of a good story, such as appealing characters, interesting settings, clever plots, detailed descriptions, surprises, and twists.

Explain that, as a class, they are collectively going to create a new *1001 Nights* story that begins with this line:

One day, Shahzaman was walking through the market with Maymoon on his shoulder. Suddenly, Maymoon started jumping and pointing at ...

As the teacher, take suggestions from different students and suggest some of your own to create a story in class.

ACTIVITY ONE: CREATE YOUR OWN 1001 NIGHTS STORY...

Now that you've seen (or heard) a number of 1001 Nights stories, it's your turn to create one. Here's what to do:

1. Begin your story with the following paragraph:

After a long journey at sea, Sinbad and his crew found themselves on an island. Noticing something gold glimmering in the sand, one of his crew cried, "I think this place is Treasure Island!!"

2. Write an outline that tells the big picture of your story. Who is the main character, and what do they want? What exciting obstacles will get in his or her way? What other interesting characters will come into the story? How will the story end? How can you add humor and suspense to your story?

3. Write a first draft of the story and read it aloud to a friend. What did they like about it most? What would the friend recommend changing?

4. Write a second draft of the story and add pictures.

TAKE-HOME ACTIVITY

NAME: _____

HELPFUL STORY HINTS:

When creating a story, you may want to think through some of the following questions:

· Where does the story take place (setting)?

· Who is the main character (their name, age, job, family)?

· What does the main character want?

· What gets in the way of the main character's goal (obstacles)?

· Does the main character overcome the obstacles? If so, how? If not, why not?

· What are the main character's strengths? (What is he or she good at?)

· What are the main character's weaknesses? (What is he or she not good at?)

· Using just a few words, summarize the beginning, middle, and end of the story.

TAKE-HOME ACTIVITY

NAME: _____